History and Its True Colors

History and
Its True Colors

Poems

Tanure Ojaide

SPEARS BOOKS
Denver, Colorado

Spears Books
An Imprint of Spears Media Press LLC
7830 W. Alameda Ave, Suite 103-247
Denver, CO 80226
United States of America

First Published in the United States of America in 2024 by Spears Books
www.spearsbooks.org
info@spearsmedia.com
Information on this title: www.spearsbooks.org/history-and-its-true-colors

© 2024 Tanure Ojaide
All rights reserved.

No part of this publication may be reproduced, distributed, or transmitted in any form or by any means, including photocopying, recording, or other electronic or mechanical methods, without the prior written permission of the publisher, except in the case of brief quotations embodied in critical reviews and certain other noncommercial uses permitted by copyright law. For permission requests, write to the publisher, addressed "Attention: Permissions Coordinator," at the above address.

ISBN: 9781957296302 (Paperback)
ISBN: 9781957296319 (eBook)

Spears Media Press has no responsibility for the persistence or accuracy of urls for external or third-party internet websites referred to in this publication, and does not guarantee that any content on such websites is, or will remain, accurate or appropriate.

Designed and typeset by Spears Media Press LLC
Cover Art: "Tobore" by Bruce Onobrakpeya
Cover designed by D Kambem

Distributed globally by African Books Collective (ABC)
www.africanbookscollective.com

Dedication

These poems are dedicated to the memories of Patrice Lumumba, Ken Saro-Wiwa, and Jamal Ahmad Khashoggi. They left no bodies to be buried, but we remember them, and they live on.

Contents

Dedication	v
Preface	xi
Acknowledgments	xiii
MOVEMENT I	xv
Betrothed	
Let Me Never Tire You	1
At the Behest of Aridon	3
My Vessel	4
Because I Trust My Muse	5
O Aridon!	6
Aridon Always Pulls Me Aside	7
Betrothed	8
MOVEMENT II	11
The Idiot Has His Say	
The Idiot	12
My People and I	13
Distances	14
On Both Sides of the Atlantic	15
Home-less	16
What I Can Do	18
Abuja Suite	19
If We Knew All	21
Warri & I	24
At the Beach, On My Birthday, 2022	25
Return Home	27

MOVEMENT III
Still Waiting — 29

Elegy for the Elephant	30
The House of Clever Fools	31
They Would Rather	33
#EndSARS*	34
In the Land of Anger	35
Still Waiting	38
Seeking Friendship	40
The Enormity of Sacrifice	41
When the Rogue Elephant Falls	42

MOVEMENT IV
For Earth, Our Only Home — 43

My Creation	44
Lament of the Forests	45
Homage to Earth, Our Home	49
Boyhood Intuition	51
Another Earth Day, 2022	52
The Stranger	55
Sighting Deer in the Neighborhood	57
Loving	58

MOVEMENT V
Love — 59

Prehistoric Love	60
You Wore No Mask	61
In the Invisible Army	62
Birthday	64
Let's Beat the Beautiful Drum	65
Okamuka, My Love	66
Love Riddle	68
Do This for Me	69
Messaging	71
So Simple	72

MOVEMENT VI   73
Their True Color

My History Book	74
Orukuruku	75
Colored Neighborhood	76
Their True Color	77
So, This is History	78
History's Habits	79
Police Protocol	80
Their God Is Something Else	81
They Were Once Demigods	82
Forgiveness	83
Waiting for Mass Conversion	84
Vignette	85
If Only They Knew	86

MOVEMENT VII   89
Intrepid Tales

I Wake	90
Others Bring Us Down	91
The Marathon Runner Limped Through the Finish Line	92
You Missed and Won the Election	93
Atlanta-Charlotte	94
Discovering the Backyard of Discoverers	95
Let Me Not Forget	96

MOVEMENT VIII   97
Other Histories

The Year of My Birth	98
Another Eclipse	102
Nembe Kingdom	103
The Sitting Figures of Esie	105
Remembering the Penny-a-Year Oba	110
Benin History	111
Christening Grace and Rob	112
Peace Poem	114
May the Days Be Far Apart!	116

MOVEMENT IX
More Histories — 117

The Cry: From West Papua — 118
Landing on Empty Land, Captain Cook's Style — 119
Remembering Edinburgh, 1979 — 120
Let Me Dance: A Monologue — 121
Trending — 124
They Deny Racism — 125
English Semantics — 126
Greenwood, Tulsa — 127
Berlin and the Unforgivable — 128
History's About-face — 129
Bill Against Lynching — 130
Reparation Blues — 131
Redemption Song — 133
What Becomes of History? — 135

Epilogue — 137
Poets Nowadays — 138

About the Author — 139

PREFACE

History and Its True Colors is the poet's reflection on history from the multiple positionalities of creativity and self, personal relations, society, nationality, race, humanity, and life, among so many dimensions. The collection is in nine movements, each focusing on an aspect of history. The first five movements touch on history in a tangential manner. "Betrothed" examines the relationship between Aridon, the deity of memory and song-poetry, and the poet. In "The Idiot Has His Say," the poet-persona wears the mask of a fool to reflect on self and others. The "Still Waiting" movement contemplates mostly national socio-political issues and the quest for a savior. "For Earth, Our Only Home" focuses on the imperative of tending the Earth whose condition rebounds on humans. The "Love" movement is on human relationships. The latter four movements are more directly involved with history. "Their True Color" movement is on history that connects the rest of the world, especially the West, and Africa. "Intrepid Tales" relates to the Coronavirus-19 experience. "Other Histories" and "More Histories" critique writers of history in their subjectivities from local and national to international perspectives on issues of truth, racism, wrongs done, and the necessity for penitence, reparation, and redemption.

The nine unique and yet interrelated movements do not only memorialize the African past but also represent the journey to the past for its remains still affect human experiences today. It is a past that has not fully passed because the past and the present are connected and capable of shaping the future. On a personal level, the poems reflect a journey within and without the life experiences of the poet. The collection ends with an Afterword.

History always fascinates me. It makes me sad but also gives me hope. Somehow, with time, it resolves its own contradictions. In a broad sense, history here has to do with memory at individual and collective levels. The lessons of history are germane to human experience and development. History matters. Individuals or people have a better sense of their future direction if they retain memories of their past experiences—avoiding past errors in confronting current adversities towards a better future. History is to me a mirror through which human progress can be envisioned. Human progress is not made up of imperial conquests or material acquisitions but a selfless understanding that one life should help others in a good neighborly relationship.

Poetry writing is a verbal art that possesses me like a spell, which, when spellbound, takes me through different emotional and ideational landscapes. In this collection, I observe and harvest from the abundant fields of history a poetic essence that I believe will make humans more humane and accommodating of not only fellow humans but also nonhumans for a more harmonious habitable universe. The passing years have saddled me with history and I have unburdened myself in the poems that follow in nine movements.

Tanure Ojaide
Abuja, Nigeria, and Charlotte, NC, USA
November 30, 2022

ACKNOWLEDGMENTS

I want to thank the University of North Carolina at Charlotte for several small grants that gave me the resources and space to complete this collection. I am grateful to Funso Aiyejina, a fine poet and literary scholar, who carefully read the poems and made comments that helped me to arrive at the final version of the collection.

MOVEMENT I

Betrothed

"When the wind blows,
the wiregrass dances."

(from an Urhobo folksong)

Let Me Never Tire You

Aridon, let inspiring me never tire you.
I have gone far with words you presented to me
but still have further to cover to break through.
Let your gaze never leave me. Bless me
with what it takes to be the *owena** of songs.
Possess me to move the world into frenzy with rhythms
that no one can resist even with wood in their ears.

You thrust me into this circle for which many abandon
chores to come to share and cheer the beauty I have seen.
I keep on breaking records, sacrificing to you.
I am your favorite; let the world nod to the songs
you present through your sworn devotee.
Guardian of words, your abundance is infinite;
let your inspiring me daily never tire you.

I still strain for metaphors to tell stories.
Muse extraordinaire, help me compose songs.
I do not have all the sonorous notes I need
to strike a magic chord and raise a lilting voice.
Many may have heard me at home and abroad,
but still much of the globe remains untouched.
Aridon, let inspiring me never tire you.

I cannot tell if the book I start writing with a riddle
will be completed with the correct answer for the reader,
and if its every fragment will tell more than the whole.
I cannot see far ahead and you have to guide me
from the dark to see the unseen. I need divining eyes.
Let every call to you always remedy my malady.
Aridon, let inspiring me never tire you.

The more the *otie* tree advances, the juicier

---

* owena: an exceptionally magnificent master-artist in Pan-Edo folklore.

the fruits it proffers its host community.
The divine delays menopause in the one
chosen to bring forth the hero to deliver the people.
Let the years add more verve to my songs
composed beautifully and sung mellifluously.
Aridon, let me never tire you.

At the Behest of Aridon

No sooner done with one timely task
than Aridon dares me with another errand.
I cannot rest when Aridon calls; a summons
strikes me with a fever I must answer to feel fine.
Divine blessing comes with a special call.

I want to bring the quotidian into my song,
deploy metaphors and riddles to capture small things;
I want to see and hear what those at home are doing
to fend off the perennial monster rather than give up
the good life and freedom that are their birthrights.

There are many small things that should guide us
but we are abandoning them for grand gestures
that stall us from the goal we set for ourselves
that the constitution revises and rewrites
into green and white paper that can be shredded.

Aridon sends me to sell small things of virtue
that we should hold as a charter of faith
in place of the big things that keep us down.
And so no sooner done with one task
than Aridon challenges me with another.

My Vessel

I come with an empty vessel to Aridon
whose spring overflows with a rare elixir.
Many boast of gathering dogs' tears in gallons
which can't match what the spring's drop brings to life.

I am no longer a supplicant; I come
assured of the benevolent abundance.
I come with an empty vessel to the spring
Aridon keeps beyond the reach of desperate seekers
but there to bring the favorite to draw from.

The spring is not far but cannot be seen or poached.
I come to the mystic spring, stare at the abundance
that eludes so many but my flood to draw from.
My calabash takes away from the inexhaustible stream.
I take enough draughts for this suite of songs, knowing
too well there is always more for other times of need.

Because I Trust My Muse

These pages of poetry I write day and night
bear the brunt of wildfires that I fight to tame.
I walk around and nobody notices what is wrong
with one carrying unbearable heat on a calm face;
eyes see no bleeding wounds but I am drained.
I can be crazy but not explosive to self-destruct.

I commit my challenges and yearnings to poetry.
Let verses absorb my lamentations and celebrations;
let my pen transform into pretty lines those worries
capable of impairing me from the flow in which I live.
One needs to channel away perilous flames or floods;
there is a sea out there waiting to consume my anguish.

And so tears of pain and laughter, tidal lows and highs,
drench an entire page and more without drowning me.
I sleep under threats of a tornado without shaking
because I trust my muse will take care of me.
Aridon is always ready to take the bullet on the chest, knowing
that a god will not suffer mortality from weapons fashioned by
men.

O Aridon!

Keep me from benefactors
whose generosity will fix me
to live on charity and wait for succor.

Break that friendship
whose company will shield me from those challenges
designed to strengthen me with a stubborn resolve.

O Aridon!

Close for me thoroughfares whose crossroads
incur accidents that mar the journey or take me
where I will be unable to take the right turn.

Save me from adventures into the unknown
that do not open new vistas into the world
I have always sought but not yet seen.

O Aridon!

Close the shortcut to the destination
that is doomed to fail to reach my goal
but open the longer route to safe arrival.

And let all my problems not be solved
since even gods can't yet untie every knot
so that I remain human, struggling, hoping.

Aridon Always Pulls Me Aside

I wonder why Aridon always pulls me aside
when the group or crowd is ecstatic or depressed
at the course or outcome of so many happenings.
Am I responsible for individual and collective actions?

I have no right to be in front or at the back
and deny complicity; it matters not if others are
sandwiched between me and my shadow—
I am part of the cobra; head or tail dangerous!

If I keep mum to a hate speech, I'll be guilty
of the victim's lynching. If I speak out loud
against a lone voice that is gentle but enervates me,
I am part of the throng throwing one into flames.

Aridon asks many questions. Can I take responsibility
for all the deeds of the crowd I lead, follow, or hide in?
Can I happily be part of the sacrifice I propose for a cure?
There is no excuse to save myself at the expense of others.

I have learned not to be carried away by coups for which
my compatriots brandish green branches and dance deliriously.
I have also learned not to be depressed by the depravity
of many humans out there since others stand to save us.

I cannot question the visionary god who has more
than my sense, sees better than my cataract-free eyes;
he hears the needle drop on sand I shake from my shoes
and feels the storm before dark clouds blindfold the horizon.

So I let myself be pulled aside from back, front, or
center of the group that carries me in anger or joy
to look beyond what makes my people happy or sad.
Aridon warns me to act alone, not be swept by waves.

Betrothed

Nowadays, poetry makes up for all that I lack, drives me
to overshoot distances I was once too handicapped to cross.
I do not need heavy accounts to count me as comfortable;
I can be light and still be the envy of property owners.
My footloose imagination runs on high testosterone
and I am betrothed to the demanding divinity of songs.
I won't fail the caste I mortgage lifelong to remain a member.

Mockers smack my shortsighted eyes with sand and set
street urchins to pilfer and pillage what is left for me
but blind to hustling I still pick words that uplift me.
Nobody knows how I counter adversities with songs.
Bad mouths hurl insults at me from their spleen not for
my inability to climb palm trees or jump across creeks
but for their claim that the priestess and I stripped in the shrine;
the sort that turns the world upside down and demands exile.

The adrenalin does not just rush when the muse appears—
frequent tsunamis provoke me into an amphibious life.
Nothing else matters when she appears without makeup—
I flee from those smothered with wigs and fall before her.
I am possessed, transported into an undiscovered planet.
I am not fit for the chariot the choristers burnish with songs.
I am too down-to-earth to escape the trappings of beauty.

Her dust is diamond; magic and miracle—twin domains.
I shovel on farther from friction to achieve the promise
that poetry made to the boy born out of malefactors' sight.
The songs will not leave me alone—noise that is golden.
The summons of the muse reassures a steadfast spectacle
in traveling light hauling out the resources of freedom
whose goal gears to the spritely godhead lost in flesh.
The benevolence of the bounty saves me from borrowing.

Poetry does something to me that I cannot say in its delirium—
I cannot control it beyond the point of metaphors. What of

gifts of riddles and transformations that make an old man young?
I am here immersed in sweat when done and that's far ahead
in the proposition of partners without eyelashes, without flesh
to flash but bound in the humanity of a crying universe lost
wholesale and angling dexterously for thunderclaps of laughter.

See me for questions when the deed is done and I am
neither on land, underground, nor air. I swam across creeks
with the flourish of an Olympian in boyhood truancy.
I have built a house of words out of space big enough
to invite the world to a party. Love is the lingua franca.
Poetry converted my dream into a love fest flashing lights
and leaving me a vision of byways merging into the highway.

MOVEMENT II

The Idiot Has His Say

"The dream of one man is part of the memory of all."

(Jorge Luis Borges)

The Idiot

I know they call me an idiot.
The Warri boy whose school fees I pay still swindles me;
my neighbor beats loud the very drum he stole from me,
and the arsonist commiserates with me after making me homeless.
Since I do not curse them loud, they think I do not know them.

When others are gone to their personal jobs,
the people's idiot enters the communal shrine.
God hears and understands his incoherent prayers
and so when in drought he cries for rain,
it pours for everybody to start planting.

It is not bad at all having an idiot around
where pastors, politicians, and sorcerers thrive.
I do not mind being taken for an idiot
where everybody else is too wise to be a fool
to think of others and stave off needless pain.

My People and I

My people are known to have unflinching guts.
Nobody hears them wail however ghastly bruised,
but the fabled warriors weep in bed at night
in the hermitage of their deep anguish; they tell
no one in daylight their nightmarish encounters.

My people pound their chests like thunderclaps
to make other hearts palpitate and fail. They too
shed their share of tears in the Niger Delta rains;
these same folks who only remember the umbrella
after it has started raining frogs which they do not eat.

The battle breaks out before my people wear charms;
others bare-bodied always train for every bloodshed.
Our war cries startle those we are supposed to defend
into a stampede across enemy lines. Despite all,
our heroes die standing in the enemy's long shadows.

We plant prickly trees to demarcate settlements
and expect our fowls to lay eggs with thorns
but they still hatch overexposed chickens;
hence our skies swarm with hungry hawks.
Our migrant relatives feed proud home folks.

We borrow to celebrate alien festivals
but feel ashamed to display our inherited talents.
They laughed at me for declining a party in Dubai
for the mud-splashing Orhirhi Festival* at home.
Folks, I am what we are; they are not me, my people.

---

* Orhirhi: a traditional festival of communal cleansing of the Okpara sub-clan in Nigeria's Delta State.

Distances

Where I come from,
women used to dance the mask*
and men did the handclapping.
Grandma wore a man's top hat
to perform the *ikenike***moves
that startled the public to applaud.
Years earlier her husband had slipped.
My wife and I argue equality;
our sons and daughters, unaware
of how far we walked and ran
before them, now want to fly
to even nearby places.

    *   There is a folkloric song about Okurekpo women dancing the mask.
   **   ikenike: an Urhobo type of stilt dance.

On Both Sides of the Atlantic

(for Oladele Akogun)

My friend finds it difficult to be happy
with happenings around and beyond.
The ethnic cleansing in Kaduna State roils
his conscience as much as America's race clashes.
He spits out what chokes my mind.
Where is the humanity to be happy about?
Images from Europe bring sadness of past
savagery. Do not mind the EU's humanitarian
gestures to pay back but too little
with the litany of robberies and murders
for which they cannot even pay King Leopold's
share of debts to crippled generations of victims.

I cannot laugh in a make-believe theater—
I know the president presides over pogroms;
he sits deaf and dumb to agonizing cries.
On both sides of the Atlantic no succor;
another president summons soldiers and
police to do the deed that deals death.
You would not doubt he is a Klansman
from his utterances and exhortations.
It is difficult to be happy or laugh
anywhere on both sides of the Atlantic;
the atrocities stoked from power houses.
My friend and I are in trouble on both sides.

Home-less

I am bound to be here
from where I took off in flight.
It would have been an odyssey
if a refugee could be granted that honorific too.
I left the Delta whose rains Shell had turned into acid
to raise the Stock Market and toast power in Abuja.
I arrived at Chevron's home lit with gas still flaring
at Eruemukohwarien* beyond the pale of global eyes.

Where else could I have been now than here
if the horsemen of Borno did not throw me down;
broken bones healing from the vigor of youth?
I could not be converted to another form of worship
after I left the one in which I had served as altar boy;
I had grown not to accept any taboos dictated to me
when living on writing and reading is liberation enough.

Where be this day other than today
lamenting the hostility of hosts,
the fascism of the chieftain at the big white house;
the streets battlefields fueled by the commander
who leads a section against the entire nation
when home is no better at all
with a president embedded in a rock
and whose beliefs and kinsfolks serve him more
than the nation's constitution he scorns with silence?

Where else be than here now
home-less despite multiple houses in my name,
nation-less despite citizenship of two nations
with none to choose from at this time
and at home nowhere that should be home

    *   Eruemukohwarien: a village near Ughelli where Shell has a flow station and where gas is still being flared.

bound to here at this stage of the journey
hoping for a change to get to a stable home?

What I Can Do

What I can do
swat a fly from perching on the sore of the hand-less
stop and plant a red flag at a deep puddle
surrender snacks to the hungry

that needs to be done
before a simple sore gets infected
before a driver plunges into a pool
before the famished one faints

I have not done
because timeliness means nothing
because my energy is there for no activity
because all the gifts of resources will atrophy

always consumes my thought
and invites me to do it
because there is not always the time
energy and the ready tools

to do all I need to do
and can do
hence I am always working
and will always when I can.

What I can do
that needs to be done
I have not done
always consumes my thought
to do all I need to do.

Abuja Suite

1. Musing

The muse in silence
sharpens my ears
so that I can hear words of wisdom
amidst cacophonies of fake news.
Social media is fueling the riot
that has become a lifestyle.

It is wise to be hard of hearing
these days of antiphonies.
Right is left, far is near
and only a disinfected ear
takes in the right sense
that is left of a basket of lies.

2. A Dog Barks

A dog barks
at a shadow at night.
The curfew is holding tight
but the neighborhood is still on edge.
We are more secure
in the dark than in daytime.
The truth of an inanimate shadow
tells a worrisome tale of the time.

The wind must be blowing;
leaves and tall grass dancing
and the dog barks
when a curfew is holding tight
taking violence off the street
or, I suspect, now that Covid-19
is poaching despite the governor's
order to stay in or face consequences.

A dog barks
at a shadow at night
and its owner and the neighborhood
sleepless because the wind is blowing
and leaves and grass dare to dance
in celebration of the lockdown curfew.

3. My Silent Witnesses

At my arraignment nobody believes me.
The judges say they will be patient
with me, and they are ready to wait
but not ad infinitum for my witnesses.
How could all witnesses be tongue-tied
and with no knowledge of sign language?
I know sunlight and night see it all
as the All-Seeing in infinite vision
but comes the time for defense I am left alone
to speak for myself. My words aren't enough.
I trust the sun, trust night, trust the All-Knowing
but they leave me to acquit myself
in the court whose judgment depends
on the tongue slashing one's accusers,
or be sent to jail to converse with roaches.
My witnesses seek no bloodbath;
they do not want to gang up with anybody
and not even with me; they are too clean
for the sludge into which I drag them
knowing that the free should suffer
to understand the true limitations of justice
which the sun, night, and the All-Mighty
know too well in their serene silence.

If We Knew All

If we could know all,
we would know the unknowable.
Knowledge is broad and deep
but still expanding and so unfathomable
that nobody can embrace it with open arms
or ever reach down to its bottom.

If I knew all,
I would be a diviner
but not even the diviner is divine
enough to know a right step could be a misstep,
that sacrifice however costly could be futile.

If we knew all,
we would not be human
retarded by our nature
always pursuing knowledge
with its so many aliases
and science taunting with new horizons
that we cannot conquer, always ahead.

If we knew all,
imagine a population without prayers!
There would be no congregation to fleece
because the end would come to us
without summons, without sermons;
we would see the hidden without light.

If we could know all,
arithmetic or physics would be literature
in the anthropology of sociologists.
Everything would be generic to the letter
and originals would not matter
as the product would be the solution.

If we could know all,

where would all the workers earn their living?
When would each day take off
and pass through to arrive at dawn?
Who would be the cock, the town-crier,
without any gratitude from humans
slaughtered and stewed as a delicacy?

If I could know all,
Ananse's pot must break and scatter*
for all to acquire a bit of their own.
No capitalist thought would solve problems
that keep on mounting as some get resolved.
No school of thought would open night
to light without technology screwing up nature;
no party or sect would save adherents
from the therapy of faith.

If I could know all,
I would not be a fool
Ajapa carrying its fortune in a shell**;
a trickster celebrating a narrow escape
before being caught again and disgraced.

If I could know all,
I would not wear clothes on clothes
when birth-suit is my best outfit,
talking and talking to gain attention
when silence is my natural advocate;
amassing and amassing prodigiously
even though lightness is the blessing I need;
climbing and climbing as if I will go through the sky
as gravity watches and mocks my ascending steps.

If we could know all,
who would be a monkey and not a giraffe;
a turkey and not a dove?
Why would I be hiding so much in my thoughts

---

*   Ananse: Akan folkloric Spider hoarding all wisdom in a pot that broke while climbing a tree and thus dispersing knowledge.
** Ajapa: Yoruba folkloric Tortoise, a trickster, carrying all it has in its shell.

with desires dressed to hide their identity?
What I packed in the vault is too much
for one person to confess at the confessionary
if conscience kept tight guard of everything.

If I knew all,
I would not play games
that would hurt me,
games I could not win or lose
but must play to remain human.

Warri & I

Warri is no longer the same place to me. In youth
we played games a stuntman won't attempt today.
I somersaulted on top of a disused car tire
and kept my balance firmer than an Olympic gold gymnast.
We sought adventures waiting for accidents to happen
but always did not because of youth's unfailing magic
that assured safety in blindfolded devilries on the cliff.

Now bearing the burden of all I gathered
from decades at school, workplace, and travel
if I were to try to somersault on a Caterpillar tire,
would observers not shake their heads in utter disbelief
at a depressed man's choice of suicide in hard times?
If I taunted the cliff, wouldn't I break neck and head
that some would pick away for money-making rituals?

In Okoye Street* a miracle saved curious boys from syphilis.
We envied the outside world that AIDS would ravish
but compelled us to learn the virtues of derided abstinence.
Fame is no longer free in overrated street freak shows.
Notoriety before peers earned such enviable respect
and not Facebook's following cheering what they don't see.
Warri comes to me as I walk away from the place.

Now I am ready to "carry last"** and be triumphant
leaving Warri to its folkloric ways; defeated and happy.
Is it I or Warri that changed beyond recognition?
I am no longer Boma Boy and nobody remembers that stuff
as crafty Wafi is unable to rise to its memorable nickname.
Can I still be a Warri Boy after the countless years that
I have abandoned its wonderful staple to be an itinerant lover?

  *   Okoye Street: till the 1970s a quarter for prostitutes in Warri.
  **   "carry last": from the popular saying, "Warri no dey carry last."

At the Beach, On My Birthday, 2022

I

This is what it means to be born again
without thunderous rant,
clean without cosmetic cleansing,
bare-bodied, a tree without foliage;
body dipped in dawn's ocean waves
and suntanned on an island beach
after waking from psychic slumber.

This is what it means to be reborn
out of step with age-mates and colleagues
flowery and flamboyant for acclamation;
they have no other goals than to flaunt
titles and mansions, their accomplishments.
Of course, young women tone their dark skin
to *slay*, avow charm as trademark of success.

This is what it means to be reborn
into a start that is far ahead into the goal,
into the vortex of self-discovery as a human
capable of rubbing mud on the body to glisten;
wet when drought threatens the soil
and dry when floods disguise armies of despoliation.
It is not the position one takes to come first.

I am up to another year
without moving up or down but changing status
and no body part seeking replacement.
It is more now of thought than physical compulsion;
it is a song that seeks neither victory nor defeat,
neither sleeping nor keeping awake through days
but a matter of transformation of vision.

I am reminded of lapses and relapses
to start all over again in determined self-conquest.

I saw myself in an elevation
and had to work my way down for recognition.
I am a child again despite my elder's seat.
I am the envy of those without my fears and laughing.
Surely, I am born again without thunderous rant.

II

Today, as a novice I am riding a white horse.
I flywhisk my way through a crowd of adulators;
a chieftain leading cheers of nonchalance.

I am able to tell the moon from floodlight.
At the beach I pick sea shells as trophy
of dawn's arrival without a hitch and I was there
before sun and sea kissed, offering me courage
to do my own thing, take love to wherever I want.

I revere the sea that swallows rivers and not bloated
and will not choke from wrecks littering the waterbed.
The sea brings out dawn with serenades of waves
and I liberate myself on the exposed brave beach.

I am riding the horse whose tail I tagged with hope;
not for the fancy of phantoms but for fortitude.

Return Home

The deep wound refuses to heal outside
despite developed diagnosis and medications;
return is the only remedy left to try
but sure to change the situation.

Walk on the soil and your feet saunter gingerly;
take the food and are free of chronic health issues.
Immerse yourself in the primordial waters
and you have cleansed yourself of aberrations.

Only a return home counts in the struggle
to be at peace with oneself and others;
only acknowledgement of one's inner remedy
helps to close the chasm that inflicts the wound.

The more distant, the less realization
as I come to live the heat, laugh, and cry
amidst the indomitable tasks for change
that only hand-to-hand combat decides.

Upon arrival, the wound begins healing;
the new first steps tentative, but a great start.
I am back to the land of simple lives
whose mysteries save me from helpless conditions.

MOVEMENT III

Still Waiting

"... no prescription cures a sick country nobody loves."
(from *The Endless Song*)

Elegy for the Elephant

This cannot be the elephant we cried for;
it starves in a vandalized makeshift zoo.
The keepers feud over allowances, feed it
leftovers. There has been a change of guards;
the elephant and its trainers live in a world
that unsettles open spaces of the imagination.
In a possession dance it tramples its pack
and uproots the plants on which they lean.

Today a dinosaur mounts the elephant with style.
The rider does not intend to go far and spits along;
the road is closed and no road-maker to open it.
The elephant shrinks, a giant toad in a damp spot;
the dinosaur on top kicks the beast to move.
The wrinkled rider wears the hat of a warrior
but cannot disarm poachers from his tribe he armed.
Everything is out of place and the land suffers.

The poachers are still after the dinosaur
and the diminished hulk of an elephant—
the keepers, trainers, and poachers have
formed a liability company not registered
but thrives on the carcass of their totem.
Anything goes in today's desperate hunt.
The dinosaur and elephant are not taking
folks anywhere out of the besieged state.

The House of Clever Fools

The House of clever fools
pulls down its own pillars.
They want more of the pecks
that ruin lotus-eaters; they want
honey brewed by stingless bees.
They fantasize sex with dolls;
fragranced molds of genderless idols.
Nebulous deals, cluttered tables
without respite.
The winds blow only one way
without respite,
the fury a conspiracy of madness
without respite;
as a lopsided weight of rocks
hangs high on mud pillars
without respite.

The House stands on rotten protocol—
the avalanche moves blindly
to bury towns on its way.
Cries of anguish sweep the air
without respite;
there are tears at mass burials.
Let those without ears continue
to pick their nose with infected fingers;
let them dare to pluck the leopard's beard
with the chant that has lost its charm.
The mad wind creates a path
on the land strewn with perils;
it makes a wilderness of paradise.
It has no medallion status
but badges into sacred groves.
Madness fuels the wind, the wind fondles
genitals of maniacs on aphrodisiacs.
There is no redress for a half-century
of suffering without respite; only

an emaciating populace of beggars.

It has to be a House of clever fools
pulling down its own pillars
that waits to fall from a thunder strike.

They Would Rather

There are servants who would rather beat one of them
than the master who works them to death for profit.

I have met women who would rather worship a phallic god
than castrate the serial rapist that he had been to them.

There are many out there who would rather crush you
than uplift you with the sheer weight of their power.

There are those who would rather enjoy seeing you in the dark
than give you a fragment from more than the enough share of their light.

And many would rather want you below or with them than above them
as others I know would rather hate than love me for telling the truth.

#EndSARS*

The old held their ground and made us proud
until corruption blunted their mettle
to reduce them into laughingstocks.
Where is the valor once wielded to fight
and regain what had been seized from us?
They bled as the leopard they brought down
before carrying home the prize, shoulder-high.

The youths have to start their tales of manhood
and never give themselves to their elders' relapse.
Every march moves forward. Youths march ahead;
they carry high standards singing anthems of peace.
Onward they wave their green-white-green sheets
rippling high in the air, clean despite dust clouds,
singing of heroes past right there in their column.

Then a storm of soldiers tears them down and
spatters the soil, fluttering flag, and all with blood
and stifle the anthem ringing in their mouths.
Cameras capture the shattering of a solemn march
with shots that smack everyone with shivering cold
before human burnt offerings littering the ground
bringing nightmares for the media to sharpen.

The old have come to corrupt the present
but the youths must start their history afresh.
It is awakening time after half a century's slump
robbed memories of the past from the present.
The future assembles rubbles of a proud nation.
It is awakening time and nobody wants gunfire
but salutations to freedom and brave hearts.

---

* #EndSARS: a series of youths' mass protests against the brutality of the police Special Anti-Robbery Squad which culminated in the massacre of youths at the Lekki Toll Gate in Lagos, Nigeria.

In the Land of Anger

1

They throw flames at each other; the nation, an extravagant
bonfire into which jewels of old, honesty and patience,
and invaluable beauties of the heritage, are incinerated.
We are left without a proud item to bequeath to the young.

After the people surrendered power, fireball-throwers
feel empowered to slash and burn the commonwealth.
What is left, they loot and hoard ready for a life of ritual abandon.
They indulge in luxuries in the midst of multitudes of barebones.

Everything is catching fire in our hands, the industry of decades
flared to ashes to leave nothing to assuage the prevailing famine;
the gains of independence squandered as electoral boxes fuel
anger from the arbitrary inconclusive INEC* television results.

2

When you greet someone, expect insults in return for your civili-
ty—
we spit out fire, scorch pre-historic love and friendship
and lose their essence. We have become hollow men and women;
we make noise but lack what it takes to thrive as humans.

Compliments are rare commodities; stuck with a staple of insults.
We want to wound, scald, and kill others to reap benefits.
I am angry with others who are angry with me and everything.
What's left of us, if we lose control of ourselves, lose our cool?

The land fuels a vast bonfire so intense its extravagance smothers.

---

* INEC: acronym for Nigeria's Independent National Electoral Commission that is supposed to be non-partisan but is often not perceived as so by opposition parties.

Now robbers, prostitutes, pastors, and politicians gather
to strengthen their partnership and fan the flames, devour
the country and trash what is left of candor, courage, and integrity.

They have mastered the shortchanging craft of diabolic tricksters
and they are mortgaging their lives to blow the world to ashes
to prove their prayers and policies can punish disbelievers
trying to stop them and the soporific flames from engulfing the nation.

3

Anger has pitched a vast tent over the land
after breaking loose the bile reservoir of the national dam
that now floods everywhere and half-drowns all.

Every word from every mouth provokes outbursts of curses.
Everybody is angry with me however civil I behave.
I am angry with everything and it is telling on everybody.

The pastor annoys the congregation by talking only about tithes;
not a minute on good neighborliness or helping each other;
folks are looting coffers to sow seeds for the pastor to smile.

I walk into the street or market and I am angry at humanimals
who do not mind living lavishly on dirt and condemning others
into the pitfalls of their negligence. Thieves fill market and church

with weddings and funerals, businesses rife with flamboyance.
There is swearing for robbers who laugh off others' losses.
The few good roads are bedeviled by brainless drivers.

Every police, soldier, and civil servant rotten—angry
with their state; and the people are angry with them and the state;
they are headaches to themselves, to the government and to the people.

The baby in the womb is angry at the lack of health insurance.
Bride and groom are angry; though together they are doomed for break up.
Young and old are angry at each other and at life that denies them their dues.

I rage against the land that fails its people and at people who fail their land.
I rage against a nation without any notion of nationhood;
I rage against a land that depresses its sons and daughters.

There is venom everywhere, no safety in the land;
the leaders misappropriate the abundance of the land.
How will the people not be angry and curse even in their sleep?

4

The land is angry
with a topsoil of vomit and a subsoil of poison
and not feeling the warm soles of men and women—
today is so far away from the past
when there was conviviality of all beings.

The waters are angry
with waterscapes of other beings reclaimed into land
because humans are multiplying, their desires bloating.
The fish population dwindling from avid malpractices
by those who care not if they kill themselves to get rich.
The waters miss the company of their residents;
the fishers can no longer wait for the fishing season
because life is hard for them without criminal acts.
Today is so far from those days
when each acknowledged the sanctity of the other.

The plants and their dependents are angry
at the harvests of their still green fruits
to market away their virtue; nobody
waits to give trees respite to thrive
and the harmonic orchestra of the residents of the forest
fall silent from the insane assault of men
who reduce the forests to a sand fill; a burial ground.
Today is so far from yesteryears
when we were so contented with simple needs.

Still Waiting

The epic pregnancy lingers
into fears of a miscarriage
after a half-century of a harsh existence.
The fears of a miscarriage are palpable
along the state-abandoned road to delivery
from ravages of kidnappers and robbers
capable of kidnapping the fetus for a ransom
and murdering the unborn infant for rituals.
They care not who the birth presages,
possible savior or their criminal kind,
and leaving mother and expected one
to expire in a pool of blood.

We have waited over half a century
for the hatching of a healthy cockerel.
The waiting is wearing all of us out;
the populace is losing patience with delay,
the mother a patient at home in a ward.
There is recrimination all over the land—
the midwives are not ready for a new birth,
the politicians and pastors are yet to disinfect
themselves and their congregations
from the scourge that is a pandemic of woes.
The public does not know who to blame
for the unending season of rot it thrives on.

The pregnancy persists with debilities
but when will there be a delivery?
EndSARS was silenced with gunshots still
reverberating in the caves where the fetus
sought refuge in the beleaguered womb.
Elections have become counting games
without rites of correct numbers
as umpires make pronouncements
and offer certificates to fake winners.
How long can we be living on fakery

and survive with fantastic figures as
the practice of budgets, votes, and age?
They choke the fetus of the resilient womb.

We are waiting for the hatching of the cockerel
and half a century later not closer to light;
farther away from jubilant songs than before.
Roaches and rats are gearing up for a race
that we all know will take none to nowhere
because there are no free pathways nationwide
to the refuge we seek for the cockerel.
Powers above, galvanize the living and the dead
to fight the last battle to live on or die
because the pregnancy is telling on the mother
with so many forces after the fetus
diviners see as bearing a standard of salvation
but cannot be delivered to rid the land of pollution
to make us breathe free, walk free, and live free.

Seeking Friendship

The search for friendship brought me here;
a wilderness of two-million stragglers.
I can't make friends of aliens the more I try
to embrace them the more they race away
as much afraid of me as I desire them.
I am also a stranger to them; they believe
I harbor the same perfidy in their hearts.

Traitors fill political circles with their kind;
hence my uncertainty at making friends with those
whose ideology cares for only self and nothing else.
I seek friendship from everyone but I am afraid
of rogues, prostitutes, and dissimulators. By the time
these are extracted from the city, nobody to befriend
except those thriving in virgin wombs or victim graves.

I am afraid of the community in which I seek friendship—
Abuja bustles with Christians and Muslims
but there is no neighborliness in the cramped residence.
The sleepless social media a gang-up incapable of condemning
followers who compliment theft or perjury as wonderful.
I am afraid that where everybody is in a hurry, none will wait
to hear my advocacy of law and order not to talk of ethics.

Nobody will forgive the unbeliever they call a hypocrite
for refusing to be hypnotized into the religious contagion.
I am seeking friendship that does not yet exist—
tricksters and opportunists win hefty awards with craft.
Everybody is setting up one-man companies that are hotbeds
of rituals that instead of bringing capital impoverish them.
Where shall I live to find friends since this is not the place?

The Enormity of Sacrifice

Defenders of the status quo mass
in frightening formations to strike;
they have a thunder brand of missiles.

The resistance army, a ragtag by all means;
those about to be slaughtered beg others
to take over their sacrifice and no volunteers
step forward to cover others with their bodies.

The diabolic division dashes our hope
when most needed to survive elimination
by squelching any gains with a backward push.

We need a dauntless one from the hatching of a cockerel
long expected since things started to crack and crumble
to smash through barricades and embrace abandoned virtues
to take on the impediments that stand fiercely on our way.

The enormity of what lies ahead threatens
with intimidation but never succumbs to the challenge
of unimaginable mass of costly sacrifice.

Let the song not die; let resistance feed it
with the implanted steel of confidence to overcome
to live through overridden spaces.

When the Rogue Elephant Falls

When the rogue elephant falls,
let those who did not open their mouths
against the tyranny of rampaging power
but calculated the price of words they uttered
not come out to declare themselves our liberators.
No, they would not be in the celebratory parade;
those who had relished the privileges of the party
and not only shared the loot of the commonwealth
but also eaten at the banquet hall of state robbers.
They enabled the elephant to ravage the farmland.

When the villa and other houses collapse
from their victims' flood of tears and blood,
let those who hedged their bets
not declare themselves an arm of the revolution.
Let those who brought reinforcements to vandals
by filling social media, papers, and cable television
with interviews in which they took no stand for change
sheltering in war with those inside a garrisoned rock
when others were homeless and swamped in denials
not claim any role in the fall of the elephant.

Let the tricksters not forget what they did
and wear the joyous garment of the tortured
after the fall of the elephant and the House.
Don't commiserate with the homeless families
of the country you scorched to amass your wealth.
When folks steeped in suffering wake from their nightmares,
let those who contributed to their heartbreaks
not come out and stab the air with their infected hands;
let them know the tearful public saw them hand-in-hand
and despise them as much as they despise the rogue elephant.

MOVEMENT IV

For Earth, Our Only Home

"The earth is ours to plough, not to plunder."
(from Niyi Osundare's *The Eye of the Earth*)

My Creation

I am created from forests and creeks
whose natural magnanimity
should sustain me for a lifetime.
I was born beside water that never dries
and evergreen plants whose celestial canopy
holds back the excesses of sun and rain.
They are the mirrors measuring the landscape
I crisscross; they are my dreams, my hope.

I have grown to look to forests and creeks
as deities and yet my people disrespect them
by cutting down wood, exporting their soul
and filling water spaces with homes that will
be swept away when the big flood comes.
I cry out to them to end the massacres but
they defend themselves as making a living.
How do you wipe out your ardent nurturers
and still expect their resources to sustain you?
I know I am created from forests and creeks
whose flourishing lives sustain my own life.

Lament of the Forests

1.

My land roils in turmoil. Gnarled mastodons
and AK-47s distort the familiar topography.
Where there are no gas flares or oil spills left,
poachers infest and devastate the greenery;
the heart of the forest gnawed by humans
brazenly littering it as a right of movement.

Some of our people need meat as their staple,
since incapable of piscine or vegetarian diets
and so have to host Fulani cows for life's sake.
Wherever the tree population is dense and green,
herdsmen claim freedom of entry to build dens—
they maul the pristine body of the forest.

First, they bleed the heart and then eat up the flesh
and drink the juices in the name of free access.
They have antidotes for snakebites; they grow up
fighting lions in the savannah and fear no leopards
and other beasts that should make the forests fierce.

At the same time breeders and hunters in the wilds,
they still steal into towns for more supplements.
The land roils in turmoil. Gnarled mastodons
and AK-47s terrorize the green topography.
And here I am thinking I was having a bad dream
but I am wide awake; a refugee in a civil war
trudging with all I can take of my belongings.

2.

They have forced the forests into the hostility
between those to whom they are providers
and sacrilegious marauders flaunting ethnic power.

There is a bizarre dance of the forests; many feet
not plowing but poisoning the abundant fruits.
Kidnappers violate the terrain; the plants forced
to witness abominations astonished and numb.
Positioning for power, they first enter the forests
before pouring into towns to startle with conquest.

As if other beings have no life, they conscript
the forests and their animal population into their force
even though these have no hand in their matter.
The poachers and host communities are bending
to breaking point the forests' timber backbones;
they are forced to be casualties by those whose
police and army are more corrupt than rotten cows.

They have forced the forest residents into
the lethal fray; those without blood are bloodied
to give those without tongues a bad name;
they have no hands whatever in the matter.

3.

Forests are too godly to form their own resistance army,
too humane to spill blood;
too magnanimous to reject fugitives or to give them up.
They are the earth; they keep all beings alive;
good or evil, they deny none as children of one mother.
It is a risky existence nowadays for forests that remain;
their lives are racked by those who should be human
but demonize those who live in peaceful coexistence.

The forest inhabitants are stripped of cunning, they think
no evil and act no evil; too affable to shed blood of poachers,
and so rich they deny neither side their lavish resources.
Too godly to form a resistance army for self-defense
and now contested by wanderers and hosts fighting
their race and political battles deep in their bosoms.

4.

This assault on the forests defiles
the sanctity of groves and farmlands;

it distorts the benevolence of a providing population.
What worse insult than to tear open the earth
so assured that neither they nor those they dare
cannot sacrifice cows for a peaceful state?

Flight into the forests as refuge stations
when they are not even freedom fighters!
The miscreants mock Mau Mau's heroes
whose spears brought independence to Kenya;
they challenge Egbesu's call to his boys*
to cover their land with their bodies.
What affront to the history of fighters!

They wear out women and men to walk
deep into the forests—puncture hearts and lungs.
Dirges of silence stifle tendons of life—
that is where a multiethnic orchestra used to play
night and day; they sow fire seeds of fear
and in place of cheerful faces, masques of terror.

Marauders trample and riddle farmlands with camps—
there they rape mothers as if they have none;
they tear wombs of girls as if they have no sisters;
they bury kidnapped boys alive as if the demise
of their age-mates does not remind them of what
could also happen to them in the wobbling world.

The forests are damp with blood, not rainfall.
And to know the abode of providers, the vast
dispensary for healing every possible ailment,
and broken the reserve of humans' constant allies,
it is a shame folks know not where they should go
rather than breach the civility of the other population.

5.

Why can't we leave the forests alone?

> * Egbesu: god of war among the Ijo people. Egbesu Boys: these are devotees of the god and they fight for resource control and against the environmental degradation of the Niger Delta by multinational oil and gas companies.

Do not soil their names with blood!
Do not impugn evil in their nature!

Surely, the survivors of human wars
will inherit an unwilling accomplice.
What a pity after all the litters and bloodshed!

Do not vandalize the forests!
Survivors will have them as partners.
The nonhumans make us more human.

Homage to Earth, Our Home

From the beginning proffered residence
that had all it took to thrive, live
with the abundance of a gift home.
The list of resources unending;
the residents blessed and tasked
to keep the inexhaustible forever theirs.

Gardens, rivers, lakes, and a rich soil
for different occupations and lifestyles—
when it rained, you were at home;
when it was hot, you felt at home
and whatever season you lived well
because home was vast with supplies.

What could safeguard plenty than
the grass to graze animals, the forests
to forage for fruits that keep one fed.
There was no imbalance in population
and humans as they adjusted themselves
from tilting things into a disrupting extreme.

Our home, the earth, stretches beyond
our portion into other connected portions.
This we would discover late but still act on;
that one's happiness should erase another's
sadness and we should be each other's keepers,
and the earth is our only home to nurture.

Where the end is not known, the home
should be the permanent refuge and provider
to hold on to with care and thoughtfulness.
Let no one abuse or be indifferent to the one
whose security sustains every life
to thrive in a chain that binds all beings.

And so we could rescue the other

if in trouble as will be done to us.
Life thrives because of the earth
whose breath makes us human.
One home, one global family
to cheerfully sustain all of us.

Boyhood Intuition

I caught a fish so special
it carried most of the rainbow's colors;
its shape an inspired creator's trademark
with unforgettable patterns of different lines.
So adorable the day's first catch entranced me;
this magical beauty called *Erhuvwudjorho**
captured me, the fisher. O beauty that more
than compensates for other inadequacies,
I was awe-struck by the vision before me.

Eating it would trash a divine masterpiece
and selling it would be the ultimate betrayal.
Not just a fish but a being of the rarest wonder.
I was also a being; only a human setting hooks
or casting nets in freshwater streams around me.
If I caught a water goddess, would I take her home
or let her go back to her world? Wouldn't my blessings
increase for liberating than keeping her a captive?
I was not one to ruin a masterpiece.
So, I threw my invaluable catch back into water.

* *Erhuvwudjorho*: a tiny awfully beautiful fish. It literally means "beauty more than compensates for size."

Another Earth Day, 2022

1

Another Earth Day arrives
after high-profile summits and conferences of public pledges
of noisy nations vying to outdo each other in slashing carbon
emission, eliminating fossil fuel, and affirming eco-friendly behavior
while at the same time of the Glasgow photo ops
the English slyly open new coal mines breaking their public vow,
the Americans, to recover from plummeting ratings, lift ban on
sale of methane oil they know will bring smog to choke citizens.
Worldwide oil prices rise and Saudis and Russians want it higher
by cutting supplies for egocentric reasons; they care not for the
Earth.

The Earth suffers backstabs from champions
promising succor but poisoning the great provider.
It is always the maximum profit in their calculation;
not another's well-being, not even the Earth's survival
that capitalists worry about. It is always an about-turn
from the impressive state seal-decorated podium's rhetoric
to win standing ovations for greening on global screens;
the lie they continue to reiterate every time they meet
for state banquets and not for the abused Earth
as another Earth Day arrives.

2

Earth has become so depressed from constant abuse.
Multiplying hurricanes tear through familiar and fresh alleys.
Furious floods drown river basins of towns and farmlands
as drought litters skeletons on baked soil; a macabre masque.
The Earth has become frenetic from depraved romance;
the human callousness rebounds with calamitous reprisals.

O Earth, we implore you to be calm and forgiving

as we shout out those undermining your health;
they care not because of their unquestioned power.
We will be more determined to hold back the arms
of those whose greed diminishes and ruins you.
Your beneficiaries suffer doubly from your abuse
as another Earth Day arrives.

3

The trees flare from careless tinder.
So many beings on land hedged out of their abode
and waterscapes poisoned, rivers reduced to sludge
as any open spaces are reclaimed for construction
to meet demands of the steaming real estate market—
the Anthropocene runs berserk and so hurts the Earth
and we all become casualties of our own making.

4

Earth has been lied to, backstabbed; exploited
beyond reason and sacrificed to capital. Clogged
by greed, asphyxiated by fumes to bring out gas
for cash, the Earth gasps on life support.
The summiteers are not straightforward—
the politicians really care not if the Earth lives or dies;
what matters is whatever brings electoral victory.
From the avarice, hypocrisy, lies, and sadism
there will be no time left for the Earth to flourish
until there is more sacrifice and humanity among us
who benefit from the tolerant provider's abundance.

5

We need no reminding that it should be every day.

For who provides for humans, without whom
we cannot survive, let the spell of capital
and only-me not damage our reciprocal bond.
Let us restrain our savage appetites to allow
the generous Earth to flourish in peace
so that we can thrive in our only home.

Let every day of the year be Earth Day!

The Stranger

My memory mocks me.

What a difference it makes to transpose beauty
with ugliness, cleanliness with clumsiness,
happiness with hopelessness! Memory endures
all the seasons that came between then and now—
a luscious garden has become a bewildering wilderness.
There is no resemblance between my distant home
and my current habitation though the same place!

In my lifetime, not a distant history to the elders,
the entire landscape turned into something else.
The beauty my memory burnishes with nostalgia
blighted by cavalries of progress
and yet we have not really moved forward
nor into a better life with security or comfort;
we have merely exposed ourselves to more perils.

I am a stranger to my memory's familial home.
I tapped rubber that lived on till new knives bled them
to death and others executed to make way for flats.
Boyi, Godwin, and I caught fish in freshwater streams
that prospectors reclaimed for expensive plots
and left me with farmed catfish that tastes like cardboard.
There are no more electric fish, mudfish, snakefish—
the teeming fins wiped out by gluttons and Gamalin 20.
Hyacinths and oil clog waterways to expand the wasteland.

My memory lives in a paradise that has been trashed
by capital capers into a home without homeliness;
a tropical forest bereft of its splendor of standing trees
and only mud and sand to trail the pathfinder.
We can reclaim streams but not recover our garden
that made us happy and healthy—we learned skills
to kill our neighbors that used to be good company.
I cannot recognize where I grew up fishing, playing,

laughing, and always buoyant with life around us.

Of course, we moved from villages no longer alive
to the roadside for ease of traffic and light from oil
tapped from our veins for outsiders to thrive on.
That was the beginning of losing home
to make money and forfeit the virtues that made us
guardians of our heritage of honor and truth;
that was the beginning of the free fall of our ways
that brought us to abandon what made us specially human
for a new order that is at variance with our peace.

My memory revives me.

Sighting Deer in the Neighborhood

In the Birnamwood neighborhood,
the herd of deer live on the margin—
they forage when there is no traffic, human
or vehicular, in the doldrums of silence.
I sight them only at an unusual hour
when I take early dawn for a walk.
They are not seen in the same place;
each of the three sightings a rarity.
At that lonely hour, one or two are
first stunned, then stop for a second and,
without a backward glance, prance ahead
into the thin border habitat
between streets wooded by design.
They come out to exercise the free
movement that every being deserves.
Perhaps their feed is not enough and are
forced to eat leftovers in trash buckets.
Their dignified prance enamors the early
walker who stands still gazing at
their familiarity with the area—
despite fences, never does any get stuck
as they saunter to their secret abode
in the green we leave between rows
of homes that squeeze them into
the margin to live precarious lives.

Loving

Of course, I was already flirting before I knew it.

My first love was a butterfly in the forest farm;
it appeared with flourish and then disappeared.
I fell in love with the evergreen with a lavish headgear—
it was not fazed by drought as floods regaled it
and it kept its position minding its business all the time.
I went crazy for the *otie* cherry's ripe fruit which still
falls to me when primordial hunger for songs attacks me.
I chased the sunbird for more than its plumage and tune—
its spell brought me to be lost in the heart of the forest.
I loved the deer, long-legged and sleek, that I would learn
transformed into even more translucent beauty at night.
I fell for the fish whose acclaimed beauty deprived it of size,
and by then a polygamist I sought mudfish whose contours
put sex into my head before I knew what adults did in love!
I continue to fall in love with so many in my neighborhood.
I love them living outdoors and I easily fall for them.
After I lost my innocence to the sorcery of human beauties,
till today I compare my first loves to the later-day ones
displacing what had been dear and still so dear to me.

Of course, I flirted for long before I realized it.

MOVEMENT V

"I don't know . . .
what a lover's destiny will uncover in kisses or tears."
(from "*First Night of a Broken Heart*")

Prehistoric Love

(for AND)

It is prehistoric love: total self-immolation
that surpasses human understanding of this age.
Emotionally clawed, you would rather not tell
not to bother another with thoughtless reprisals
when you loved to choking point and kept mute
to the other for whom you suffered strangulation.

Stoic queen in the bronze-cast throne of honor,
breed of endangered womanhood, you are divine
not crying out and withholding the severest of hurts
not to give the inquisitor pleasure for more torture.
Graceful one more than ready to be martyred for love,
the untold anguish you suffer at the stake fortifies you.

Now, who by right should share the agony with you
salutes you for the prehistoric love with this song.

You Wore No Mask

You wore no mask to the possessing dance;
you came not as an ancestress or goddess
but one who wanted to be happily human.
You wore no mask to where others perform
with practiced surreal or supernatural gestures.
A mask cannot fit a singular face as yours
always so radiant and glowing in darkness;
it cannot be covered without dissonance.
Often naughty, you astonish feminist goddesses.
You wore no mask where others costumed
in fetish tinsel on social media exhibit
gibberish that sells posted on Facebook.
Your phonetics mirrors commonsense carriage
without doubletalk; only straight talk that
shies not away from the heart's wellspring.
You wore no mask to the conclave of two;
you even beat back expectations—not skilled
at anything more than the ordinary; no boasts.
You also asked if I understood the riddle
of loosening bolts in a blooming body.
I took in every draught to remain expectant.
You wore no mask to embrace me; happy
to be human in the possessing dance ahead.

In the Invisible Army

Nobody can put you down by flaunting his phallus.
High time all the self-built prison houses
or those erected by self-proclaimed lords
collapsed from confrontation for a free state.
You can cut off the tyrant's sole weapon of threat.

You are just one in an army bristling in the shadows—
the arboreal growth covers you from the frontal view
of half-blind patriarchs overconfident of their vision.
Show you can steal into them and turn into rubble
their heritage of man as god; almighty but impotent!

Your thoughts and moves scare and delight me.
I can by virtue of what I share in biology be victim
but I am happy I can be the human beneficiary
of what you can give to make me semi-divine.
Love cannot scare; it will only embolden you.

There was something you hid deep beneath
your eyes, lipstick, and hair-wrap; something beautiful.
You are a rugged fighter in a hidden army
and nobody can wave a phallus to crush you;
you know that cannot ever happen to you.

I will not take your face for granted; your smile,
lipstick, covered hair, and calmness—you are
the calm of water, deep with undercurrents.
There is much wealth beneath; a therapeutic spring.

You will only fight for your peace, you say.
What a philosophy of life; what wisdom in youth!
And so you have picked this battle
rather than the many others; you harness your resources
and make meaning of life where others find none.

You can be perceived and treated as an underdog

but be the enviable sovereign of your own world.
You are queen of your life and your imagination;
standard-bearer of fortitude to strip fear from life
and live to your heart's content rather than be dead alive.

To not complain but live quietly
among those discomforted by others' wellbeing,
you make your life whole despite threats.
The monkey lives safely in the same forest with leopards;
the swordfish flinches not in crocodile-infested waters.

Let the council of elders and female cohorts pronounce
what they want, give orders to cower underdogs.
You remain the sovereign of your body. Fight for peace
and be the envied one, neither oppressing nor hurting
but amassing the peace others cannot get in their silence.

Constipate them with green berries
so that they will not enjoy the paradise of love
and not come close despite their fake supremacy.
Leave the ripe fruits for your favorite
to taste their hallucinatory sweetness.

You drive a tank through their patriarchal dreams
to smash their delusions. Who owns four wives must be
a slave master whose mules will not allow him to have peace—
he will wake into a nightmare and surrender what
pre-modern traditions gave him without your consent.

Who stunts others only hurts himself,
and let no one take in so much that kills.
Let the forest bloom for all trees;
every being deserves human rights.
I learn from you to fight only for peace.

Birthday

(for Jite at 50, on March 7, 2021)

Making 50 in 2021 is an immortal act.
Benevolent gods have kept you from slipping
in the panic of last year's tic-tac-toe.
Where you are, neither young nor old, challenges
the horizon ahead—your record this far
should take you through the uncompleted road.

Turning 50 brings you to the palace of ageless stars
where your determination fuels the race for success.
No longer do charm and talent alone count; experience too.
You know you will not run farther than the end of the road
but how soon break records that made forebears heroines—
how you can pull through perilous spots and unstopped.

Now you have clinched 50, you have to argue less,
talk less, quarrel less, and even less of every diet
you took so much time to set up as your staple.
You will practice more reflection, more assertion,
more of trust and loyalty that elevate the truth
that you speak without wincing or mincing words.

This is 2021. The zodiac so sprained that in 2020
it unraveled the world we were so used to as history.
To get where you are has been the task of mortals.
Love is now a ripe cherry that falls, never plucked;
an act so divine your minstrel arrives to sing
with a full-throated voice; gratitude for your being there.

Let's Beat the Beautiful Drum

Tonight I will make you as happy
as you made my day; I will not tire in the task.
You winnow mine to enjoy the best out there;
I will watch yours and leave you the smoothest course.

I will walk as fast as I can, match your spritely feet
not to be abandoned in the low country of expectations.
I have over the years moved the line further and beyond
till you devoured miles without sweat or losing breath.

Now I need more than my match to bring out my stamina.
I met you silent but seeking a sojourner to go very far.
Be unbearable so that I can learn to take bitter leaf as sweet;
be harsh to me so that the cruelest weather will drive me on.

I am hardened because we bruised ourselves beyond tears
and no other challenger will get away safe from our blows.
You sifted away the sand and chaff that would nag me;
I placed in your mouth spigots of the spring I discovered.

Today, make my day as happy
as I made your night. After failing in false starts,
let us beat the beautiful drum we strung over decades
to dance the new steps we discovered deep within us.

Okamuka, My Love

1

Wonder why I find myself in a prison
whose doors are open and without guards?
Night goes as far as taking off the roof for me
to converse with the stars that bother not
if I flirt and dance away with their queen.
And yet it is a prison where I seek God
in a different direction from the dome
and I am sure to find what my heart wants.

Love beckons at me through a backdoor
but I know I cannot liberate myself without
being caught in the waiting arms of the muse.
I trust many desires gathering to consume me
and I need to remain calm in the storm they provoke.
What brought me into confinement also takes me out.
I am not freer in the crowded street than indoors
where I enjoy no privacy because my desires
flash through me and create needless buzz.

Not only love brought me into this coop
with the doors so many I can be lost
at exits that had been entrances.
I learnt to segue, living in and out.
Every relationship is a clinic I visit—
many mend broken hearts to a fulsome state
while others make the malady worse off.
May what I seek bring solace! Let whom
I seek not bring *okamuka*; more worries
than I can handle to live with as a human.

2

Every entrant into the grotto brought headaches
that super doses of Codeine could not cure.

A beauty sought my ride only to hand me over to robbers!
Many liaisons became sources of wracking pain
but a single one has more than made up for my follies.
There are folks like me who are afflicted with a malady
that leads them to prison and back, and there is
nothing you can do about it when it happens; humanity
for you is not watching birds pecking at each other—
you are free or captured; concurrent giving and taking.
Why did I invite an estranged friend to my house?
To reopen or close wounds that refused to heal?
Hope drives humanity to fall deeper into commitment
or come out of it; a state that drives us to rise or fall.
My love so far has been what my people call okamuka.

Love Riddle

They are sinners for falling in love. Not in line.
They go to exorcize themselves at an altar
where there is every reason to be irrational.
Their memory measures with an irregular rule—
when it is their desire, they get there in a flash
but there is no inkling of movement forward
when summoned for sacrifice to assist others.

Two actors keep to a distant tryst on time
because they are driven by the same storm
lashing inside them, heading for safe arrival
where all roads take the pilgrims light at heart.
They arrive prepared to clear litters of long ago
for a highway to the festooned city of adoration.
They know what fills the head and seals the mouth.

Do This for Me

Regulate this tongue spilling out words
that bring disjuncture to partnership.
Let your gift words mend the fracture.
The chick shouldn't be scratching hard ground
while the cockerel lounges in a lush garden.
Let your retinue of healers come to my rescue.
After what slips out to exercise freedom but hurts,
only from you can I seek what to make amends with.
Aridon, do this for me.

Aridon, let your words be music to straining ears.
Pluck the thumb piano's metal keys into a flourish
to mend the bird's broken wings to fly into blue skies.
Summon seaside breeze to escort my guest ashore.
I have not come to collect home beach sand or weeds
but for someone staying away but waiting to come in.
Stir the waves for a splash on land of the water maid
that shakes off salt bubbles to display coral splendor.

O metal hand piano, play on
Aridon's serenading tune for me
to rouse the chick from the hurt that shakes her.
O pen that scribbles divined prescriptions,
open the infirmary of words for this need.
O page with which Aridon wraps gifts,
let this script be bandage to frayed nerves;
do this for me now that cries for solace rack me.
O tongue, roll out Aridon's minted words
to ease the flesh that suffers the deep tear.

Aridon, this is my call to you.
It is also my call to one hurt by my words
and who needs to step back from rage.
A call has a destination to be summoned to.
Bring me whole the chick of the sprained ligaments
in a flourish to one lost in new life's music.

Minter of words that heal and possess,
the one who gives high taste to tongues,
Aridon, do this for me.

Messaging

The secret message I pass to you daily
always slips through into your heart;
it escapes the strictest policing.

What is a secret to you who knows me wholesale?
What is the message other than what I do not say?
Who messages encrypted feelings waits for a response.

At dawn I rush to WhatsApp to check
if the night has sprouted a garden somewhere
I can withdraw into to relish and be lost for the day.

Or does Facebook recover in superb photos
what I tweeted on beach sand counting memories
for waves to deliver to you in a fantasy palace?

The sleepless night has raised fierce storms
and the day's relentless alleluia enthralled us
with echoes of the heart's beat; waves ashore.

Silence does not guarantee this secret.
The urgent message I pass to you daily
might not, after all, be that secret.

So Simple

It communicates without opening its mouth.
It is not taught to anyone.
It is understood without being spoken.

I remember my elementary school days
when I wrote letters for big girls to their boys.
I thought I helped them light fire
but the real excitement came when boy and girl met
in a lonely path and their eyes stuck; incredible passion
that pen or tongue did not carry. The body sent a telegram
without wire; received at both ends with fever,
each trying frantically to put out the other's flames.

Decades later I realized I had wasted time
and acted against my instincts; calling daily
to plant my heart in the other's; as if
incapable of life without another's voice.
But what would work like a diviner's spell
came out differently. I speak silence; or rather
my silence is so eloquent it works wonders.

This particular language is so simple
but many proclaim it loud in vows
that the wind disregards passing through.
We only look at each other's eyes
and know that that thing called love is a witch
we do not see practicing her craft
but turning us into beings needing no efforts
to reach the clouds and float away.

MOVEMENT VI

Their True Color

"The conqueror writes history."
(Miriam Makeba)

My History Book

What they do not talk about
more than fills my history book.

They start not from bush raids of armed liveries,
they mention not the murders and lynching parties;
they have no sentence for partitioning other people's lands.

They do not tell their children
the taboos, the rapes, and robberies committed;
all that greed drove them to do—

acts that disabled others into perpetual cripples,
the burning of cities and looting to cart away
treasures that harbor the souls of millions.

They will never tell in their books
the unforgivable that racks the conscience;
they will never own to the perfidy.

I am more interested in their unsaid,
the unwritten *orukuruku*,*
than the charities they flash today—

severed hands for the sake of rubber and ivory,
lacerated backs of cotton field workers in the sun,
and the unutterable they refuse to tell their children.

What they do not write about
more than fills my own history book.

---

    *   orukuruku: Urhobo for misdeeds.

Orukuruku

Where I come from we call it *orukuruku*.
If against the Commandments of whom you serve,
you cleanse others' land of its people,
call proprietors of a land fauna and flora,
and shoot at them like game for sport
committing what you damn know is murder,
all the evil one could imagine perpetrated
but exceeding the wildest imaginings
in the pursuit of other people's resources
we call that orukuruku where I come from.

It is orukuruku we call it where I come from
if you throw an innocent person into jail for life
because you want to advance your career and care
not about right or wrong, throw someone into jail
because he is *black* and *they are all criminals*.
You speak the unspeakable and watch with glee
the lynching of a fellow human being as a picnic
or follow police protocol to kneel on one's neck
and remain unmoved by public shouts to let go,
that is what we call orukuruku where I come from.

We call it orukuruku where I come from
when you are damned by your own rules.
It is no small matter to one with a conscience
breaking the public's established code to abide
by the self-restraint of the strong among the weak,
share the world with others but not conquer what
belongs to others or appropriate all as one's own;
the abominations that nobody wants tagged
to their names, with perpetrators forever haunted.
That is what we call orukuruku where I come from.

Colored Neighborhood

As I take my daily walk in the neighborhood,
a splash of the wood's colors cheers me up
even as politicians of the South insult *colored* people
by whatever subterfuges of election reforms.
Diverse shades fill my heart with warmth.

Colors are so natural to the eyes
but conceited humans manufactured codes
and labeled people with them; each group
with what those quick at naming called them,
as if humans are black, white, yellow, or red.

I grew up far away from here admiring colors
of plants, fruits, birds, fish, and animals
for the beauty they add to the world.
Nobody was called by a color name;
all people human among other beings.

Europe exported its invention to the rest of the world.
I am happy Apartheid died after conflict of colors.
America's Christian conscience tormented by colors;
Brazil complicates colors to absurdity,
and indigenous peoples suffer worldwide for their *color*.

Abroad, I was branded *black* from the airport
by hosts who did not hide their hostility,
inflicted pain on others to produce wealth;
the only thing they know too well to manage
and proclaim supremacy as if they are not human.

The colors of nature in my neighborhood
contradict the human practices for which
many people still build lives around codes.
Colors are natural and should not be coded
to defeat the beauty I enjoy in my daily walk.

Their True Color

They wear solid pink all over
but they say they are white.
Kaolin is white but not humans.
We know their true color.

They knock this into their heads
and so live the very lie
of what they say they are
but we know their true color.

So, This is History

So, this is history
we have seen exposed,
stripped of its heavy make-up;
the beautiful language of imperialists
covering savagery with heroic make-beliefs
sowing flowers over bloodstained soil
to lead audiences through false gates
and sing nationalist songs
for the gory actions for which
they stand accused and accursed.

This is history
having no conscience
inventing a god they call Almighty
to lead their charge afield into massacres
and a litany of gruesome deeds
that the metropolitan writes into heroism;
unprecedented savagery that will rebound
someday, some year, some age to come.
So, this is their history
written large over unhealed wounds.

History's Habits

History astounds me.
Despite hiccups and stutters,
perilous or smooth turns, and foggy lenses,
it creates an inexorable path.
It confounds me with its capers.
Despite redactions of deeds and misdeeds,
it still fills vacuous vaults
of inexhaustible documents.
History astonishes me
with its clumsy but sure mass movement,
often linear and cyclical, tardy and impetuous.
Despite cover-ups and revisions,
retouching racism and savagery
into nationalism and patriotic duty,
it is an omnivorous snake
casting off its old skin for new.
It confounds me
despite the plans and plots,
the unimaginable burden it bears,
it moves inexorably on
with so much untold and written
with the same reality
that is so subjective to either side.
History astonishes me
with reverberating proclamations
and only conquerors are too shortsighted
not to see the rubble that will take over their empires;
only fools foresee history
not resolving its own contradictions
however long it takes
in the timeless time left
to live on degrading and restoring itself.
History always dumbfounds me.

Police Protocol

They shackled a paralyzed man
to a hospital bed in Kenosha;
the police said *We are following protocol.*
The same police that shot at a man's back
seven times, assassination style. Hunters,
mobsters, cultists, who? The police!
They shot a man leaving after mediating
where two women were having an issue
and whose three children in the back seat
were on their way to celebrate one's birthday.
The police said they shot him seven times
point blank on the back going into his car
because there was a knife inside the car.
What prescience told the head hunters
there was a knife and not children?
Later there were camera shots of Kenosha PD
treating supremacists with water and high-fives
following the protocol of the police force!
And they would leave an out-of-state teenager
free to roam the street and plow down two.
And yet in the hospital bed
the police shackled Jacob Blake
because theirs was to follow protocol.

Their God Is Something Else

Their God has to be something else;
the grand patron that mass murderers
invoked to cleanse a land of residents
and to occupy as their gift refuge on earth.
For this, they have annual thanksgivings.

Their God has to be something else.
I refuse to worship the slave-owners' Lord
who condoned savagery of blood and tears
to break his chattels into perpetual zombies
and nodded at hymns for the *good* fortune.

Their God has to be something else.
I would not enter the temple
from which they exclude other races
and where their God guides their action,
cheers them to shoot those who look different.

They tell me we are all God's children:
those relying for a living for centuries
on armed robbery and killing for wealth;
their only path of sustenance, bloodshed.
Surely, their God must be something else.

They Were Once Demigods

Only from so far away could I take them for what
they were not. I would have declared them gods
from a distance but fortunately, I read and travel
and it takes living with them to really know them.

If I had not lived among them, how could I have
torn off the glorious mask that dressed them as heroes
instead of bands who hunted simple folks for sport;
how would I have known the depravity in their heads?

I live among them and know them closely. If one could meet
the hawk in its nest, one would discover its deprivations—
the famine it constantly suffers in the heavens, source of
human yearnings, to make it swoop to the earth for chickens!

It is not as told in the movies; Hollywood retouches—
the poor pathetic; the mass depressed citizenry
and capable of terrorism and worse things.
Lines of hungry folks snake around skyscrapers.

If I had not lived among them, I would have remained
fooled to invoke a god without a godhead;
I would have been a stranger to their world as they
had forced themselves as hosts in my homeland.

They have not yet canceled the iniquities they rode
into knighthood and sainthood. History has all along
been a masquerade without a god as guardian of its charter.
It would take a lifetime of penitence to pay for the sacrilege.

I would not have known the hoax that history is;
I would not have seen through the theatrics
in proselytizing a godhead empty of truth.
I would not have known their true color.

Forgiveness

I

How could one be so unforgiving
after dehumanizing centuries,
still unforgiving of slaveholders?
How forgive the unforgivable; calculated
acts to cripple others into permanent helplessness
and to create a paradise to extol the loot of power?
Why would anyone go that far in villainy
to contort justice and still be human?
Why go that far to wipe out others
too feeble to raise arms against aggression?
I remain unforgiving of injustice.

II

What ocean will wash bitterness out of me
so enraged by centuries of vandalizing
that I invoke Iphri* to scorch the torturers?
I pray to be forgiven for not forgiving
after giving enough time for recompense, and
still no penitence for centuries of rampage.
Forgive vultures but never the murderers!
If I manage to free my hands from chains,
why not hurl thunderbolts at my enslavers?
Let us keep the lord in a hot dark cell to taste
sour bread and beg for forgiveness for his past.

---

* Iphri: Urhobo divinity of revenge and restoration.

Waiting for Mass Conversion

A witch breaks ranks to confess deep secrets
to redeem a dishonorable name. A robber rats on
another to give up the loot crushing his conscience.

How many tortoises will outlive their longevity
in an island or well of change to absolve
the hunchback tribe of their terrible tricks?

Youths bring down Colston's eye-arresting statue
and roll it down dirt into Bristol Harbor; they acquit
themselves from the slave merchant's orukuruku.

Even those we often insult as not going far enough
deserve a nod when we discover they are not cast in infamy
by a single act of renunciation of their own past.

A wizard burns down the community's coven
to make refugees of torturers in the dark.
All is not lost in the task of stopping doom.

Many are already fugitives from their grandfatherly laws;
they see better than befogged spectacles of their inventors.
They are breaking ranks but not yet a multitude of converts.

How many vultures will turn on each other to devour
themselves out of existence? How many break out
of secret societies to give the rest of the world peace?

A sliver that is a lifeline stays there to spirit through.
So, it is not a damned house without any openings to air
if we can hear cries of remorse from among the inmates.

Vignette

They loosen the rope
off a dead goat

to tie down a living one
for another sacrifice—

there is no reprieve yet
for the victim population.

If Only They Knew

If only my people knew
what history hid from them,
the servitude bedazzled in globalization,

if they knew what they should know,
if they knew the alphabet of pain,
they would sing songs of sorrow
and not Liverpool's football anthem.
If they walked through the gate of no-return,
they would wake from a nightmare
into knowledge of what they should know.

If they saw the shackled, tear-soaked,
in the plantations of history books,
if only they visited the museums, crime scenes,
cemeteries where ghosts howled for vengeance,
if they retraced the fugitive path
reddened with dog bites of reprisals,
if they knew something and not nothing
they would not second-guess a goalie's punch,
join delirious waves of fans
or kick the air as if on the field;
only if they knew…

If only they saw through the football stadium
beyond the hat tricks, the goalie's dives,
the sudden death and hooligan fans,
the Liverpool slave merchant's face;
if only they knew
the stocks of the team were bought
with profit from their ancestors' sale,
if only they knew themselves
from history at home and school,
they would see shackles, hear cries of long ago
still holding them down in duplicitous diplomacy.

If they knew their history,
if only they knew who they are
and have the vision to see through the abracadabra
to liberate themselves from global shackles
in today's blinding light of Liverpool's Stadium,
they would not shout deliriously
and helplessly in Accra, Lagos, or Harare
who should know and shut their mouths.

If only they knew
and have memories of knighted merchants
and their slave cargoes,
they would not disrespect heroes
who plunged into the Atlantic deeps
rather than be sold to raise capital!

If only they knew,
they would remember who they are
and what disablers did and still do to them!
If only they knew.

MOVEMENT VII

Intrepid Tales

"Once the boat capsizes, its recovered contents are never complete."
(from an Ohwahwa udje song)

I Wake

Another day breaks
into the familiarity of rites,
and yet happenings near and far bring together
the fear and joy we share and cannot escape.
Things get more familiar; fear
fiercer than ever and we seek ways
to bring the day to nightfall.

In quarantine every tick-tock
awakens to chatter and tears.
Those who narrowly escaped fatality give thanks,
as if others caught surrendered themselves
and not the same God's children like them.
Dead or alive, we have all become casualties;
the littlest of beings cuts down populations

but we still wake
from sleep that we crave for
in the season of mass burials.
Respite from fear is only a bite
to tame hunger, a drop to push back drought;
movement to postpone permanent slumber.
Tomorrow may not know its own secrets.
The arrhythmic heartbeat intensifies,
as I wake to complete another day's command.

Others Bring Us Down

You would expect
that with the world driven to the brink
and everyone scared of the plague
in its ruthless war, the trauma dire

we would, despite social distancing, masking,
and following secular ablution protocols,
have the other's back to stay safe
and keep life triumphant over death

but lo, schisms of all types intensify
to an insane hostility. Sit-tight presidents
throw fuel at the doldrums of party politics
and political cults grow to the detriment of democracy;

the greed to take advantage of others
and build wealth makes the population callous
and you wonder if we could love others as ourselves
if the taboos we break to amass more would not crush us

instead of protecting the dying species
and growing the human genes with love
there's a cantankerous storm lashing at us, not the virus,
laying ambush we can avoid, if we have each other's back.

The Marathon Runner Limped Through the Finish Line

(for Amreghe)

A marathon runner, she turned as sparse
as a lady could be at her animated age.
And that is besides being a disciplined vegan
to avert the excesses of meat and keep her card
of the Humane Society in good standing.
But youth was no armor against Covid-19;
a poacher without respect for anyone.

The first attack came as a surprise so easily
repulsed, the positivity looked like a hoax.
But then lightning struck the same person
a second time and it was no longer a plaything
in the ICU on a ventilator with life hanging
on a cliff for several gasping hours.
The phone call at 2 am was a thunderbolt
to awaken me to life's perennial vagaries.

I could have only updates, no visit and I had
to hunker in chants of our forebears—*she is
too young to be an ancestor and that should not be
as senior siblings, parents, and grandmother remain*!
What a prayer to command fate but it worked—
soon out of the ventilator breathing on her own.

It took months of rehabilitation to heal her bruises,
body and mind, in a few days of infection. Imagine
she, who wiped out distances, never out of breath!
She lives and that is the joy; the marathon runner
limped back from the crossroads of spirits to settle
with us rather than leave. She received our ovation.

You Missed and Won the Election

(for Amreghe)

You had planned to fly in
to cast an early vote and return to DC;
perform a crow's touch-and-go task.
But, as in some of such highlighted schedules,
you could not come to execute your heart's desires
because you caught it. Coronavirus stopped you.
It was the only subject of the election—
who could best stop the plague.

You reached the existential crossroads where turning
right, left, or upward meant disappearing into the void.
How would you on a respirator not scare us?
But a call came the following day to say you were off it;
breathing on your own. That steadied our hearts.

The feverish jolt took away your memory
and as you came along and called us,
your first concern was how you would vote.
We cannot vote for you but we can vote your sentiments.
You are learning early. Not all plans come to pass.
We are fortunate you pulled through the poacher's attack.
You missed voting due to no fault of yours but we won nonetheless.

Atlanta-Charlotte

(returning from an international trip)

You de-boarded the plane into an eerie landscape.
For sure the grand poacher had done its havoc
of scaring and killing wantonly in God's Own Country!
The airport loomed a deserted hub of silence.
It took no time to get through empty corridors, shops,
and trains to speed through a war-ravaged milling city
with abundant relics of casualties staring at you.
When I left a month ago, I did not envision this chaos.
I walked into a boarding plane long before the scheduled time;
the plane serene and no smiles from hostesses trained to smile.
I took heart to count only eighteen occupants of the B717—
a tenth full of passengers escaping to a refuge in the doldrums.
The flight over the thickly clouded skies shorter than normal
as the captain broke through a blanket of clouds that almost
covered the runways. And so much relief back on terra firma
despite the trepidations that made the heart pound like a boxer.
If Atlanta was ravaged, Charlotte was battered and so lonely—
this was not the airport where I had started my trip; de-hived!
Faster because of a few left to pick their items from the belt,
we were soon on our way home with little or no traffic.
It hit me that the driveways in Birnamwood lined a crowd of cars.
What else than folks working from home and many who
either lost jobs, retrenched, sick, or schools closed;
everybody shaking from the virus's power settled indoors
rather than be exposed to the merciless raid of the leveler!

Discovering the Backyard of Discoverers

The lockdown has made me a discoverer
in my neighborhood; unlike those that homeboys
led by the hand to where they *discovered*.

Each day's walk peels off films to see clearer,
and today, my latest find in a familiar universe
of winter performing its cold rite on beings...

I discover the truths and the lies on which
life is built to be seasonal or perennial;
each canceling out the other but both there.

In the midst of the nude population stand
evergreens self-absorbed in their difference
defying winter's power to strip—

they give the majority arboreal residents
what to look up to in verdure; a costume
invaluable to procure in the cold season.

In the midst of these naked plants,
evergreens that show how desperately
the temperate seeks the tropical.

They are not many wearing green in the landscape
but populate winter to avert death—each according
to its virtue. Many green climbers clutch the nudes.

Winter does not prevail over every root of being
before forces of life take over the universe.
Stubborn hope to rebound or not bow at all!

The lockdown has made me a great discoverer
in my neighborhood; not like those that our
homeboys carried to where they *discovered*.

Let Me Not Forget

Let me not forget the trees
that kept me company in the lockdown,
the trees I had time to so admire;
their nakedness a model without makeup.
They never tired of standing
and waiting for me to pass by them.

Let me not forget the trees.
Each outing gave me a fresh vision
of branches that would rather soil themselves
than allow the trunk to fall flat on the ground.
The trunk invited squirrels as the branches
and leaves welcomed birds of magical colors.

Their skin, a texture so unique it has no equal—
every design of the master craftsman, nature,
that enraptures with bareness that uplifts.
You cannot go through the wood without
getting lost amidst its beautiful constituents.
Each chooses a cover; thorns to smoothness.

Let me not forget the trees.
They did not forget me in entombment;
they stood there for me to count on them
to remain alive rather than be boxed in.
My neighbors, they always cheered me up.
I salute the trees that stood firmly for me.

MOVEMENT VIII

Other Histories

"It is unfortunate that the dead know not what goes on."
(from "Kogho," an Ohwahwa udje song)

The Year of My Birth

1. Born After the End of the World

You could say it, not to my elders' surprise,
that I was born after the *end* of the world!

The year I was born came after a solar eclipse
that my people took for the end of the world.

Jehovah's Witnesses had warned door to door about fire
awaiting those not yet converted before the Armageddon,

and my people, who had believed the world was a snake
forever rejuvenating despite age, succumbed to the alarm.

And so, as the sun in brazen afternoon wrestled with the moon,
these simple folks looking up to the sky for protection saw

their proverb of the sun and the moon never meeting disproved
by higher powers they could not comprehend and so feared.

In the ensuing overpowering darkness, according to Grandma,
many folks trembling confessed loud their transgressions—

those who stole unsuspected spoke out, as those who made love
outside their marriage homes, and other self-condemned ones.

But true to the wisdom of ages the proverbs always proved right,
the sun soon threw off the dark cloak that tried hard to smother it

and daylight lavished the world with smiles and sighs of relief;
the youths snatched drums from racks to beat jubilation tunes.

I must have been born a year after that sign no villager could read
because there was no science to interpret what none had witnessed.

Am I the offspring of that dueling couple, each returning to its

traditional role
or the son of one who had lost boys now calling a boy a girl to
protect him?

You could say it, not to my elders' surprise,
that I was born after the *end* of the world!

2. Palestine

It took British and American troops to secure the port and land
for the regrouping of scattered tribes to take place in Palestine

where others already claimed sole ownership of the land they
had shared but, not expecting old neighbors, took as only theirs.

The new refugees that were born like me that year still live
under tents that discriminate against them as outcasts on their
land.

But Dafetanure and Avwerhoke* knew not Palestine; they
knew not Jews and Arabs, nor the conflict that birth inflicted;

and so, in the year of my birth I remember them all in Palestine:
the Jews that need to be home from persecution and Palestinians

who should not be refugees in their own land—they can all live
on the same land that can happily accommodate them as neighbors.

My birth demanded a song of rejoicing for the gift of life
but the child cried, unsure of the earth it had come to grow in.

3. India

India was also born in the year of my birth, a quadruplet
whose ancestors had been there for eons; battered but standing.

From the dominion of Moguls to the British, no conqueror can
forever outlive the destiny of a proud and endowed people.

---

* Dafetanure and Avwerhoke: the poet's father and mother.

From different capitals through the Red Fort of the Moguls,
I see the other civilization that capitalist invaders saw not—

they carted away gold and so much produce from the profuse sweat
of the vast land, but they could not cart away the spirit of its folks;

they gave orders to be bowed to but the bow fooled colonizers to stare
at palaces and lessen their guard over the people's indomitable spirit.

The year of my birth was born a cat nobody foresaw would pounce,
but today strides with the pride of Asia to contend with in a new world;

today my age-mate invites me to celebrate the resilience of 1948
and parade before the world at 70 the blessings that have come to light.

4. *That Year*

Only that year after many prohibitions failed to stop profiteering masters
came the Universal Declaration of Human Rights to put a stop to slavery,

only in the year of my birth did the savagery in the name of religions
come to be exposed: the eunuch in Jeddah, the chattel in American plantations,

and millions dispersed as far apart as China and the Americas;
helpless ones on whose blood and sweat others thrived as lords.

Only in the year of my birth did they put an *end* that was no end
to the many slave names in the lands of those who preach freedom

but live on binding others to untold misery. Despite the year of my birth
royal chiefs still hide slaves in their flaring robes of flatulent affluence.

Until Mlozi* was hanged, how could the Makonde** have peace?
Not until 1948 nowhere in my land was safe haven from raiders.

Until the year of my birth and after, in Sudan and Mauritania,
my kinsfolks did not cry; they had no tears left to express pain.

Only in the year of my birth did the world, despite thousands
of temples of different faiths, wake from the insatiable greed

that plunged my land into a nightmare that still traumatizes the mind.
Thanks, that robbers had a change of heart and made these gestures

from the year of my birth. But we still wear scars of Tippu Tip***
and the many deformities inflicted on the ascribed color of my
skin.

---

*   Mlozi: callous slave raider who assisted Arab/Muslim slave traders in East Africa.
** Makonde: ethnic group in East Africa mostly in Mozambique.
*** Tippu Tip: notorious Arab slave raider in East Africa.

Another Eclipse

(on the total eclipse of the sun in parts of the United States, August 21, 2017)

Next year another child will be born like me
a year after the total solar eclipse; not in the village
of terrified folks who believed the world had come to an end
but in a city of clear-eyed ones to whom a predicted eclipse
will be a treat to see nature perform one of its major stunts.
Unlike my people caught bewildered by the eerie appearance—
the oldest had neither seen nor heard of the sun-moon tango—
these Americans are already preparing for the next coming
when those to be born a year later, like me when ours occurred,
will be old and distant enough from the scene of excitement
knowing the lifetime experience will shift to another region
so far away that only the rich in a cruise ship will capture
where darkness and light will be one; nothing to seek
when bearing children will not be a human task at night
but a lab to reproduce birth and prolong life as we know it.
After this centennial display of nature's rare side of discord,
folks now out to watch it as soon as it unfolds and disappears,
unlike my people startled headlong into a sinister ambush
but like them after the wonder will go to the tasks of life
and a year later will bring forth children of a generation
very like mine—offspring of partners capable of discord
but settling for their separate roles to have peace at home.
A year from now another child will be born like me
in the spirit of a sun drowned in darkness resurrecting.

Nembe Kingdom

History thrives on conflicts, if not outright war,
and the internecine goes into the people's chronicles.
And so a Nembe* minor could not wear the adult crown
and his uncle was asked to rule on his behalf; a regent—
an interim arrangement whose future nobody predicted.
When the regent died and the prince demanded his right,
a fight ensued with his uncle's son claiming the kingship
as his own right and they tore apart old Nembe Kingdom.
In the existential struggle, climaxed with imperial cannons,
the bridge holding together the river-bisected island
blew into water and Nembe was no longer one state.

Nembe remains two kingdoms of one ancient dominion;
two islands of one kingdom; the compounds belong to
two: Nembe Bassambiri and Nembe Ogbolomabiri. This
was reconciliation Nembe style—let there be two kings
where only one used to reign over the same people!
Today by state law two kings rule there first-class chiefs:
the new smaller and compact side of the renegade crown
and the larger, older, less populated side sprawls with legitimacy.

Today whenever a council chair is elected from one side,
the winner moves with the headquarters to their side of town;
the other then provides the vice chairman, a balancing act.
And the two halves of the original kingdom share historical sites—
mausoleums of Mingi and Ogbodo sons, princes and pretenders;
cult centers on both sides that formed the judicial centers of old;
and spaces set aside for communal social activities that make
life have a rhythm that no two kings could disrupt with orders.

Nembe's history from the beginning rested on water, allied
now to Aboh to free the Lander brothers, then to marine Brass
to bring in a new religion from afar, the Nembe Bible, and schools.

    *   Nembe: an island kingdom in Nigeria's Bayelsa State.

They set aside in the renegade kingdom a quarter for medicine men.
History carries the dividing river in its broad heart and today
centuries of rivalry and coexistence in which the CMS School
of the old town produced professors for the rebel side to represent
the Nembe constituency in Abuja and be the people's mouthpiece.
A new bridge is contracted out to rejoin Nembe; millennial spirit.

History surely has the patience for quiet diplomacy to testify
to the slow healing of the deep wound it inflicted long ago
though memory remains sharp with a trail of landmarks
of history, the triumph of the two sides of Nembe Kingdom.
Now a new bridge rises where the old one fell from; the new
expected to be impregnable to war assaults and schisms
with ancestors and water spirits spectators and guarantors
of a new pact that will bring back regattas and water sports.
The state pours in not just concrete but the power to make
Nembe the ancient kingdom of only one ruler, the Amayanabo.

The Sitting Figures of Esie

1.

I will go to Esie* and there look at folks in the eye,
in the daylight of the savannah clarity of distances

not muffled by films of harmattan haze for excuses
and point at the figures nobody remembers making.

I will go with a frenzied mind to the home of wonder
and interrogate living residents who cannot take me

through proverbs and folkloric routes of the heritage
to the last thing to forget—their bequeathed pride.

They cannot remember creators of the cache of treasures
sitting there unrelated to any history of rampage or blood.

I will go to Esie and there not only marvel at wonders
of those who had preceded the living but left them

a talent kilned in the furnace of ancient civilization;
the renown that comes with such primeval wealth.

I am on the way to Esie to unlock the brilliant light
pinioned in total darkness to question the mystery.

I am not going to Pompeii to recover the molten;
no frozen stream of lava or ash cloud in the vicinity

to have buried alive thousands of artistic progenitors;
they all lived, children after parents in unending lineage.

---

*   Esie is a Yoruba Igbomina town in today's Kwara State of Nigeria with a museum of soapstone "sitting figures."

I am not going through or into excavated caves to
an underworld of spirits who once shared the land—

I would have called on Akin* to accompany me
to excavate a buried heritage and extract a tome,

exorcize the spirit of the violated silence to be
magnanimous towards the living searching for clues

but how can a people who have not moved their homes
forget themselves in the open savannah of their refuge?

Who forgot, the people or the gods they chose to serve;
who forgot, the land or its owners who created their gods

and would have invested their stories and rich lore
in daily rites that would remain inseparable habits?

I leave for Esie with horn and harp in tow on the road
to retrieve memory of days when talent was universal.

What happened that nobody remembers, that none
who participated or witnessed the tradition passed it on?

What happened that the living then locked their
masterpieces deep in the bowels of the dark?

2.

I have to go to Esie to find out the figures
where they came from to be planted there.

When came the hiatus from between the past and now,
when did they lose memory of what happened or not?

I go back to the past, no highway the artisans took here—

---

* Akin: Akinwumi Ogundiran, UNC Charlotte's Chancellor Professor of Africana Studies, History, and Anthropology, who does a lot of research excavating historical sites in the Old Oyo Empire area of Nigeria.

I have to retrace the ash trail to distances long unmarked;

not even a resting place restores, no plant to delimit
the safe way to the repository of customized craftworks.

Not even fragments of broken china through which
they delivered them there where they sit unbroken;

no trace of the skill that softened hard but clayey soil,
no blood calcifying and covering marks of bruises.

How could descendants not have known how the figures
not resembling their familiar faces stand amidst them?

3.

A civilization lost to memory,
abandoned to sloth and idleness;

all markers along the road backwards
and nobody recognizes the footway again,

the furnace of the great kiln of the soapstone
and whom the neighborly human shapes represent.

None left a story for children to sing about,
no child left a tale for grandchildren to pass on

and all the deep thoughts silted into an underbelly;
all the invaluable commodities surviving but

separated from the spirit that inspired the handcrafts
and the mental conception of the sitting figures.

These wonders have no roots where they belong;
no roots deep into this soil penetrate the unknown—

no excavation helps to unravel the mystery of amnesia;
no legends clarify the fortuitous presence of the dead

whose hands cannot be wished away with revisionist
discourse of helpless generations of driftwoods on land.

The road to Esie from the ancient to the contemporary
a wilderness of memories without substance to subsist on;

no longer a fertile ground to grow wonder crops of old
and no more a constellation to shine light on the dark.

Could turmoil have doomed their minds from treasuring;
could war against themselves have devastated their minds?

Could others far or near have created the trophies of Esie,
since they do not appropriate for themselves the wonders?

4.

The *peregun* plants* that will not die keep unending memories
but who planted the ageless ones to know what they witnessed?

How could these figures get to sit beside a giant palm tree
without knowledge of where footpaths brought them from?

The oba of the human figures sits quietly in a worthy throne.
His adorned olori** sits to his left; to the right a trusted servant.

But why worship what forbears carved from the land's soapstone
that are now mystified into God's anger for lack of remembrance;

why worship the site that today's oba no longer visits as a tradition
because overwhelmed by plenitude of an age nobody remembers?

These figures are not mysteries but carry the very habits that today
still trend female hairstyles, mufflers, and beads, and men's wear;

these figures in soapstone breathed lavishly as we now breathe
for discerning artists to represent lives of every age and gender.

I do not see the mysteries that seek their worship in a shrine

    *   the peregun plant appears in Yoruba praise chants for its deep-rootedness,
          longevity, and ability to shelter folks from sun or rain.
    **   olori: the oba's wife; the queen.

by priests to pacify the demons of the unknown among them,

I want the wonders that humans wrought out of nothing
to be acknowledged and the artists sung for all times;

I choose to go back in time and salute those who deployed
their innate gifts into these sitting figures that we marvel at.

5.

But Esie is not alone on the path of forgetfulness of the self;
the vast savannah spreads forgetfulness over its expanse—

Nok now basks where it knows not its pride rests;
its art history merely a tin mine's accident of fortune

with hardly whole terracotta figures still standing
from the bruises of mining tools after it than tin

but the soil loyal like Esie's always safeguards what is
forgotten and so left under its care for silent centuries.

Esie is not alone in forgetfulness; so many suffering
the rare disease: forgetting the dead and their gifts.

Remembering the Penny-a-Year Oba

They starved the Odemo of Isara for not switching loyalty.
Exuding the dignity of an eagle soaring majestically,

he thrived on a penny-a-year government salary despite
his beaded crown for standing by the revered Chief.*

He would not cavort with vultures in place of the falcon;
he would not dance to the ritual music of carnivores.

For him hunger kills not the brave fighting for honor
but once greed takes over one, it taints with dishonor.

The Odemo remained resplendent despite the punishing stipend;
he stood erect amidst his stooping peers of first-class obas.

Hunger for more and more kills one's self-respect irrevocably
and it happened to who *crossed carpets* for forbidden foods.

Honor abides with stamina to repulse fraudulent assaults;
deprivations do not bring down the brave in battle for honor

and I remember the errant Premier's** assaults with mortars
against the Lion of Odemo striding without ruffling his mane.

The brave one takes in terrible pangs for his revered Chief
and stands with the glory of his beaded crown; unflinching.

---

* Chief: here Obafemi Awolowo, first premier of Western Nigeria.
** Premier: here Samuel Ladoke Akintola, who succeeded Awolowo and later fell out with the revered Yoruba leader.

Benin History

So that history does not turn into a blind alley,
I visit the fabled moats surrounding Benin.
The footprints of heroic Arhuaran unaccounted for.
Visionary Ominigbo's blood sacrificed for divining truth
untraceable in the traumatized terrain of unfading redness.
Queues of vassal kings with tributes appear only in masks.
Carved for sale, queens and princesses who gave up their lives
so that Benin would forever remain glorious with male obas!
And Ife looms, a large shadow the Oba cannot shake off
at Ododua festival and to affirm the legitimacy of his dynasty.
I travel through centuries of the city's bronzed timescape
bypassing foreign visitors, intruders, and soldiers of fortune
to arrive at today's state capital, coven of political wizards,
haven of sex and human traffickers, den of robbers and assassins
so that history is not forgotten in the silt-filled moats
surrounding immortal Benin. Forever there, glorious!

Christening Grace and Rob

For generations to come, no female-born will be christened Grace
and no Grace consort with any Rob or Gabriel* in the soapstone
land.
The hiatus in the history of names not proscribed but an informal
ban;
a taboo for folks startled from slumber by a stockade of gunshots
after forbearance and revolution turned into unquestioned reverence.
Not that in my village I did not have relatives christened Hitler
with
nothing to do with another's supremacist vision of world domination.
There have been no Gowons and Ojukwus after the Civil War and
no
children called Saddam or Gaddafi after their times passed for
good or bad.
After the earthquake and tsunami all in one sweep in one nation,
history
will not relive or be written with the same names as models. Hence
no
male-born called Gabriel however angelic; no female named Grace
for the crazy love of Gucci or her phenomenal rise to Doctor of
Philosophy.

No other Grace, no other Gabriel after the firestorm; one more
than enough.
After one Grace almost consumed a nation's virtues in one brazen
blaze
of besotting dance, after youth and beauty possessed an old man
into folly,
after the lord and his dame took their meek followers for goats and
sheep,
came a suite of army guns to startle the populace into delirious

---

* Robert Gabriel Mugabe, late President of Zimbabwe, and his wife, Grace.

street shouts
rejecting the unbearable as the daily norm; the ungodly as national virtue.
And now for generations to come no newborn will answer Grace or Rob;
none to grow up to shout "I don't care!" None to defy gravity of years
and saunter on after debility and time have worn out the charm of youth.
For there will be a limit to power's longevity, a limit to the spell beauty
casts on desirous men; a limit to silence that guns break for general relief.

And for years to come, none in the land or far away no Grace for daughter,
Rob or Gabriel for son after parents witnessed the earthquake and storm
that almost buried them alive and survived a half-century of deep slumber;
they rose spritely from the dead in one cataclysmic movement after shots
and none of the living will give accursed names to their later-day children.
And not until another Grace will capture the public imagination with self-
immolation—who cares if a female footballer, sprinter, or flag-bearer?
Not until some Gabriel angel or Robert revolutionary redeems the name,
through that name cleanses a people from communal meekness and docility,
not until the name does not bring nightmares to the nation but dream love,
not until there is an apotheosis of a merciful goddess and a non-aging god,
not until an angel right-hand man devolves power to others lining behind
will there be a female child christened Grace and a male one Rob or Gabriel.

Peace Poem

Being asked to write a peace poem
for one war in which everyone lines up on either side
as other wars rage beyond the pale of cable news
tests Aridon's divine judgment in inspiration.
Who is the peace for when everyone has chosen
a side to fight for—pouring immoral weapons
to fuel the tragic blaze whose end is unpredictable.
Where do I start a peace poem in a time of war?
Stop bombing, shelling, or cheering on one side
to provoke the other to annihilate the enemy?

Being asked to write a peace poem
turns into waging war against warmongers,
humanitarians seeking the next refugees
to pitch tents for and feel good about service
from which they make an enviable living.
Is peace good for capitalists who profit from
bloodshed or for self-aggrandizing imperialists?
I am looking for the benefits of peace to warmongers
and cannot find any and my pen is fighting big powers
to stop all wars they blindfold the world from seeing.

Many are already serenading heroes in the midst of ruins;
others have passed judgment on who goes to hell or heaven
as if war criminals have not been canonized in the past.
Some are masking personal pride as national salvation.
Both sides are fighting for a peace I know is not going
to erase racism from their psyches or make the world even;
two human wars for which peace needs poems and prayers
so that the armed few will not dominate the many unarmed
and live on the wealth of the poor and call that civilized.
What peace lifts downtrodden folks to stand on their own?

Now, for which war should my peace poem be written?
Is it peace or still war where a disarmed side is dying

from the oppression of the massive force of another—
silent subdued subjects not at war against their dominion?
I write for the blacked-out wars in which the most powerful
cover their depravity; not for the war streamed live on cable.
I write my peace poem for forgotten wars of Yemen,
Tigray, Congo, other near or distant wars out there, and
perennial wars nobody pays attention to but kill populations.
We are always at war and Aridon gives me this peace poem.

May the Days Be Far Apart!

When my 93-year old mother passed on
and friends poured in congratulations, "Why?" I asked them.
"Would you prefer to have passed before her?" they asked me.
I then understood their rejoicing at my grief.

And now that I have completed her funeral rites with pride,
the same friends pray: "May the days be far apart!"
I say "Amen!" and they know wisdom has sunk inside of me.
Mom and I used to be close but let our departure dates be far apart.

MOVEMENT IX

More Histories

"The evil that men do lives after them."
(William Shakespeare)

The Cry: From West Papua

When wrinkled men and women on
walking sticks strip to cry for their land,
their dutiful sons dying in their defense
and the bodies thrown into ancestral rivers,
their tears drench not just West Papua but
also inflict frosting cold on the entire world.
Pain contorts them to reach down their guts
to pour out teardrop icicles to survive the rack.
In their blessed land armed intruders
hold them down with barbaric cruelty;
they suffer as my people whose land oil and gas
turned into a bonfire for capitalists to celebrate.
Dispersed worldwide their relatives cry daily
from the nightmare of a resource-full forest home.
Those men and women whose walking sticks can
barely hold them to the ground craving them
want their piercing jaw-collapsing cry taken
to the wider world that knows not their tale;
they are not alone pleading with strangers
to broadcast their nerve-racking cry worldwide.
The cry of old men and women pours
frostbiting cold on me, my heart wrenched.
They pull themselves up with walking sticks
naked and staring at the future with open eyes
to cry to the world that does business
with their dispossessors, their torturers.
In West Papua before Indonesia's face
the wrinkled, naked, and fettered cry
to be one day free of their impositions
and regain freedom; their birthright.

Landing on Empty Land, Captain Cook's Style

(for Adam Goodes*)

So, Captain Cook landed on *empty* land
that indigenous people had inhabited for eons
and designated them *fauna and flora* to justify
the loneliness of the land. Empty land indeed!
And so Cook's migrant kinsfolks came to enjoy
the Australian Dream by designing nightmares
to haunt others for life in their own homeland.
Why will Adam not quit the sport he loves
to keep a sane mind and care for his daughter?
It is no capitulation for him; he needs not forgive
the group that does not acknowledge its crimes
of further torturing those it robbed of their rights.
The indigenous mind seeks peace in the future
but that has taken too long to arrive for victims
of Captain Cook's landing on their *empty* land.

---

* Adam Roy Goodes: an indigenous Australian who played Australian rules football but had to retire early because of racist taunts directed at him.

Remembering Edinburgh, 1979

It pays not for a victim to be only angry, or
just forgive the unacknowledged unforgivable.
Should the victim burn down the abuser's home
or spit at the accursed face of the evil one?
I was not angry at the old woman in Edinburgh
who called me *Jimmy* to my face in the street.
I told her I am Tanure. "*Tanu* what?" she asked.
"Learn it, Miss Jim!" I shouted at her.
She dared not call me names again and later
"I like your name *Ta nu re*." That is how it should be.
"By the way, what is your name?" I asked.
"McKenzie." "Kankenze?" "No, McKenzie!"
We both got it without saying it; so relieved.
Thenceforth we had peaceful coexistence.

Let Me Dance: A Monologue

(after a 106-year old black woman, Virginia McLaurin, visited the White House and danced with President Obama and his wife, Michelle)

I never knew this day would come
but here it is and I live it

I crossed rivers of blood
I crossed rivers of tears

I stepped over lynched bodies
I lived through arson and firebombs

I ran through briars and barbed wires
I marched through rubble and broken bottles

I served jail terms for no offense
they denied me service for my skin

if I should recount all the incidents of sorrow
where and when would I stop?

For life's sake I bled and wept
now for life's sake let me dance

this dance speaks out my happiness
after centuries of blood and tears

I recovered from whiplashes
I recovered from dog bites

I healed from gunshots
I healed from obscenities

let me dance to spite death
spite death of my people

I am no longer scared of death
we live on after so many deaths

let me dance I have no more fear
I walked an unforgettable way here

it rained and rained rivers of blood
I did not drown in the red sea

it rained rivers and rivers of tears
I did not drown in the sea of sorrow

it rained rivers of sweat
I did not drown in the dead sea

I woke from nights of fire
into days of black-targeted bullets

let me carry my children along
there is life ahead of death

there is sunrise after nightfall
though sunset awaits all

I have shed all my tears of sorrow
let me pour out tears of joy

and dance from now to the end
there is no more sorrow but joy

let the dispersed family gather
let all the music-makers play on

come out with the percussive ensemble
come out with all the polyrhythms

I will not dance alone, O kinsfolks
dance with me for this day

there is no slowing down the dance
after waiting all this long

I never knew this day would come
but here it is and I live it.

Trending

The world blows so hot, animated into frenzy,
and soon dips into subzero lifelessness
until another heat wave arrives only to recede.

Juan Guaido breezed about a superstar activist of freedom
until he called for American troops to install him President,
lost every support and fell deep into oblivion in Venezuela.

So did Sviatana* with her partner's detention become Europe's
household name until Belarus dropped out of world news
and now only *Siri* easily knows the opposition leader's name.

The violence targeting girls in Pakistan shone powerful light
on Malala,** Muslim female and child hungry for education,
but fell out of sight as a graduate after outgrowing adolescence.

Now Greta*** is broadcast in all media, radiant face
of the future. But who knows where she would be
if climate pledges failed to hold back scorching days?

Someone or something catches fire at every one moment
that the media, mouthpiece of gamesters, seek to project
but soon turns cold ash after all the deafening hullaballoo.

The wise are watching, quiet, patient, and not too excited,
asking, what have we not seen, heard, or imagined before?
What is now trending will soon give way to new waves.

---

*   Sviatana Tsikkhanovsky: opposition leader in Belarus.
** Malala Yousefzai: Pakistani girl who jointly won the Nobel Prize for Peace.
*** Greta Thunberg: young Swedish climate activist.

They Deny Racism

It is not the denial of the deed that heals wounds
or removes the pain that refuses to go away;
denial digs deeper the wound and pain.

Tell me: "Britain is not racist!"
"America is not racist!" "Hitler was not
fascist!" "It is the people and not the land."

Living and dead witnesses curse the colonial century.
Remnant buffalo men programmed to die in reservations.
Jesse Owen would rise and spit at Hitler's face.

Ota Benga should not have taken his own life—
"The zoo and the fairs had nothing to do with him!"
Deniers always have facile defense at their disposal.

Who says there are no racists still out there
when those enacting legislations to disenfranchise many
deeply hate those they keep from expressing freedom?

Tell me all you want but I will not accept your lies
as my truth. I know those enjoying the pain of others.
Denial cannot clear a torturer of guilt and sadism.

English Semantics

If you say
the colonial chieftain is not a racist,
the knighted slave merchant is not a racist;
the color-coding masters are not racist, and
the one who conscripted the world's forces to crush fascism
at home but colonizes outsiders is not a racist;
it must be me subjected to inhuman treatment that is a racist!

If you say
who promotes AUKUS ethnic alliance is not a tribalist,
who spares kinsfolks the A-bomb to incinerate others is not a tribalist;
who colludes with relatives to rob outsiders and keeps mum
over his people's iniquities is not a tribalist,
who is a tribalist?

It must be me recruiting an army of the poor
and disinherited across borders to fight overlords;
it must be us rejecting incestuous marriages
and consorting with strangers that are tribalists.
It must be me sanctioning any errant relations
who violate other people's rights that is a tribalist!

English must be a dubious tongue
to call the mother of all racists not racist
and die-hard tribalists of the world something else.
The deodorizers know how to sell their stink to the world.
Of course, sugarcoating is their coinage.
So also is window-dressing. English is so sly.

Greenwood, Tulsa

The past has not passed us;
it is still in flames, hence
Black Lives Matter in 2020.
Those burned with their property
could not be buried and let go
to the paradise of their faiths;
they smart on from the hatred
and prejudice of a vile mob.
Nothing yet absolves Tulsa
from the infamy of centuries.

Berlin and the Unforgivable

It began in Berlin in November 1884.
So unforgiving, men in black suits
in a winter boardroom spread out
a cartographer's sheet of a land
of abundance and through sleight of hand
disinherited endless generations.

They calculated the high profit
of dismembering Africa.
With cold calculation on all sides,
they accomplished the deed—
strangulated the future of others
without a dissenting voice and rose
to implement the wizardry of disabling
by planting flags in their dreamlands.

They accomplished their desires,
the unforgivable deed of centuries,
and the actors and their accomplices
want it forgotten and forgiven
but it cannot; the perpetual wound
that has disabled and disinherited
an entire continent of its resources.

Berlin hosted the iniquity called
conference; unforgivable perfidy.

History's About-face

1. Columbus Day

When one first landed in America in the late 1970s,
they celebrated Columbus Day with fireworks.
I did not know then a black man captained his ship.
This millennium unraveled the *discoverer*'s heroism.
Today has de-sanctified him into a historical villain!
Papers and television kept mute as if the name was taboo;
hence his fans and venerators of a *new* world fell silent;
ashamed to acknowledge Columbus had been a scourge
to those cleansed from their land seized with impunity.
His statues have been quietly removed from public glare.
His ghost should be tried for crimes against humanity.

2. Thanksgiving Day

"Thank you, Jesus!" Thank Jesus with your deeds!
It took centuries to acknowledge what everybody knew
was a heinous blotch on history's shameless broad face.
Not that there is repentance for the past smothered with blood
but the fanfare of thanking a complicit God for cleansing
a land and shipping in slaves to create capital of their bones
has died from the ability to see all the hidden misdeeds.
Times have changed; there is no force to retain old habits—
today one cannot make God an accessory to ethnic cleansing
to avoid the embarrassment of watching worshipers
handcuffed to court for countless crimes against humanity!

Bill Against Lynching

(March 29, 2022)

Supporters of lynching finally let it pass
after over two hundred rejections and spoiler counter bills.
Defenders let go what they could not admit to their children—
their forebears' picnic of watching black men strangled.

They finally made lynching a crime in 2022
after over three centuries of criminal complicity;
let this be counted *annum mirabilis* of our time—
finally, a bill convicts lynching for its spectacle of shame.

Forgive the tree still standing from which stretched the victim,
forgive the same tree that canopied the picnickers;
forgive the green lawn that held towels they lounged on to watch.
Forgive twines and strangling ropes as having no hand in the revelry.

Forgive the sun whose smile cheered them on for the macabre show,
forgive flowers that adorned and scented the vicinity to host the crowd;
forgive the breeze whose fans made revelers comfortable in the heat
but not men, women, and children who consumed this Southern staple.

Blessed are those who shunned invitation to frolic on another's pain,
blessed are those who declined the morbid entertainment
calling out participants to acknowledge all as God's children; and
those, self-convinced, turned against rabid forefathers and coevals.

Reparation Blues

1.

And yet another terrible earthquake!
History has been unkind to Haiti
because of an unexpected victory.
Peace to Toussaint Louverture's soul!
How come revolution brings this curse?

History is so unkind to stunning success.
Do not wonder why with France's wizardry.
Haiti is not just slums, cholera, earthquakes,
and assassinations. Its upheaval the first
in the hemisphere to upturn slavery into freedom.

2.

I have no respect for some folks
and utter disdain for many wealthy nations.
They are robbers of the most inhuman kind;
harassing, blackmailing, and torturing the weak.
How many armadas make right outright robbery?
What riches from extortion make it right
to command a small one to buy his freedom
after bringing to his knees the boastful big one?
Many wealthy ones stink from their perfidy.
Wonder why Haiti is poor and France developed?

3.

Reparation is the lingua franca of justice
so that history in its continuum will self-heal
the wounds that ruptured the world's peace.
But when will the broken limbs of partition
grow back for Africa to be whole and healthy?

A day may come to forgive the unforgivable;

perhaps the broken limbs will grow back
and victims will no longer smart from deep wounds
and disability and spring forward at the pace
they were born to move spritely. Now there is
no forgiveness until reparations of a kind bring
closure; not just granting partial independence
but penance of the perpetrator brings tears to heal.

Reparation is the lingua franca of justice.

Redemption Song

(for History)

What so depressed the past with gory episodes
also elevated it to a glorious stage for celebration—
the epic victories of small ones and communities
against imperial chariots of obscene conquest
and the roll call of patriotic defenders of their land
heat the blood to surge with bravery in songs
as folkloric tales gladden the heart; charm that
brings envy to the present and lights up the future.

History simply set and broke its own records—
humans who refused to die; living memorials;
Ubiesha, saintly pontiff of Oweya, dying standing!
In adventures brave folks rescued beauties from ogres
that masked as spotless men to punish the inexperienced.
Men so loved women and women so doted on men
the world was an exciting planet of relationships—
everybody happy, the songs of daring lovers fill
our lips with a challenge to dare odds to love lavishly
in today's calculations and miscalculations.

How many Mandelas can our offspring give birth to?
How many detribalized are there North or South of the Niger?
What knowledge surpasses indigenous folk instincts?
Who is revered now as those of the past in their prime?
Is the present a shadow of the solid and glorious past
and the future, despite discoveries, only looking back
seeking knowledge to rescue itself from floods and fires?

O undying past, I hold you to my heart
and foist you over the callous deeds perpetrated
to blackmail you into a ghost of terror.
You are colorless though others paint you red and ochre
and I sing of history-inspiring feats that save the present.
The shine of the past redeems humanity

as memory lights up the present to march to the future and it is left for us to be more human rather than degenerate into savages that others pride themselves.

What Becomes of History?

1.

All of a sudden those who loved history to death
suffer a phobia for the past that laid an ambush
for their future wellbeing that was once assured;
the boasts of civilization contradicted and recanted.
Who loved to discover and decorated discoverers,
murderers who delivered death to distant places,
have found out the past adventures so horrendous,
they forbid their children from having a peek at what
their ancestors did for capital in the name of civilization—
bloodshed and the barbarism of unchallenged power.
Who flaunted history as the litany of heroes,
serenaded history as the geography of growth,
planted worldwide statues of villains for adoration
(Columbus, Leopold, Rhodes, numberless dead devils),
and renamed others after these and themselves
all of a sudden deny the misdeeds of dominion
for which the knighted have become benighted.
Those who applauded discoveries as national honor
exorcising limitations of size and lack of resources
have their past discovered from the vast whitewash
with which they dressed history to their own image.
The discoverers who wrote volumes of history books
with conquistadors of priests, popes, and saints have
been stripped of their masks and behold the perfidy!

2.

Fear not, history, you will live forever.
You will be re-written and retold differently
despite the arrogance of those who proclaimed your end.
You will continue to diminish the icons of dominion
for a free world of equity and deserved justice.
You will unmask the infestations worldwide
of those who deployed you for self-centered ends;

their statues are falling to protests, their edifications
rusting with every sunrise, and empires withering.
Their conscience suffers from an unmentionable virus
that advanced medicines cannot manage for them.
The past is catching up with so many once out of reach;
it will not be pleasant for who looted wealth from others—
who threw shit into the future inevitably meets the mess!
O history, those slaves and victims of brutal dominion
will rise in their children's children to absolve you
from complicity you had been subjected to for eons;
the future is endless for you to fulfill their dreams—
the unheard will be heard; the tomes of prejudice
will be expunged for new stories to redefine you.
It baffles that picnickers at lynching could not imagine that
their grand and great-grandchildren would not be judged;
the shortsightedness of not expecting someday being
called out by those born into hell but surviving baffles.
Now the world hears the agonies of centuries coming
through barricades of defensive walls erected but crumbling;
the world sees the savagery of whiplashes that contorted skins
into scars that cannot heal in more generations to come.
History, you have been a scoundrel to so many victims
who are rising to rehabilitate you. The future is endless.

3.

What becomes of history these days when
those who penned it in indelible ink abandon it;
those who passed it on by words of pain
can now carry their heads high and laugh;
and those who styled themselves history-makers
hide from their own children the warped past
they built out of blood and sweat of others?
They deny participation in lynching and smudge
testaments of complicity but it will not go away
and now ravages the once benumbed conscience.
What becomes of history now it has been caught
and shamed for its past of racial havoc, with
the world's eyes so open that even the past cannot
be hidden in one-sided narratives of perpetrators
self-glorifying and demonizing their victims?
What becomes of history in the endless future?

Epilogue

"Asui ine k'ovwe irhivwen" / *After ending a suite of songs, the singer takes a deep breath.*

(concluding formula in popular Urhobo song-poetry)

Poets Nowadays

Nowadays I see many poets sleepwalking in daylight.
Others canonize themselves in the cemetery of the mind
and they expect to perform miracles out of disbelief.
They battle to end the uneven world through whoredom
so that promiscuous poems will inaugurate a new earth.
They plant love in the sky for clouds to tend so that
every time rain falls they can harvest fruits of ecstasy.
They are too restless to stand still, look straight,
or even move without croaking to please themselves;
they really do not care who listens to their stutters.
They seek martyrdom or heroism of no known type.
Left to them, they would keep whining till a storm
relieves them; crying a stream of drudgery till dead.
They can be appalling as they try harder to please—
it will take a deaf and blind world to stop the nuisance.
I am only one of the lost tribe that live on a planet
whose Facebook mills with millions of followers;
nobody knows where they are heading in the doldrums
that open into hallucinating cries to keep sanity despite
the devastation none of them can halt with ranting chants.
Delirium plays such an important part in the madness.
Don't mind me, if I also suffer from the trending malady!

ABOUT THE AUTHOR

Credit: author

Tanure Ojaide, a distinguished scholar and writer, was educated at the University of Ibadan and Syracuse University. He has an impressive list of publications, including collections of poetry, novels, short stories, memoirs, and scholarly work. His numerous awards, such as the Commonwealth Poetry Prize for the Africa Region, the All-Africa Okigbo Prize for Poetry, and the BBC Arts and Africa Poetry Award, are a testament to his literary prowess. In 2016, he was honored with both the African Literature Association's Fonlon-Nichols Award for Excellence in Writing and the Nigerian National Order of Merit Award for the Humanities. In 2018, he was a co-winner of the highly esteemed Wole Soyinka Prize for Literature in Africa. Currently, Ojaide holds the position of Frank Porter Graham Professor of Africana Studies at The University of North Carolina at Charlotte.

ABOUT THE PUBLISHER

Spears Books is an independent publisher dedicated to providing innovative publication strategies with emphasis on Africana stories and perspectives. As a platform for alternative voices, we prioritize the accessibility and affordability of our titles to ensure that relevant and often marginal voices are represented at the global marketplace of ideas. Our titles – poetry, fiction, narrative nonfiction, memoirs, reference, travel writing, African languages, and young people's literature – aim to bring African worldviews closer to diverse readers. Our titles are distributed in paperback and electronic formats globally by African Books Collective.

Connect with Us: Go to www.spearsbooks.org to learn about exclusive previews and read excerpts of new books, find detailed information on our titles, authors, subject area books, and special discounts.

Subscribe to our Free Newsletter: Be amongst the first to hear about our newest publications, special discount offers, news about bestsellers, author interviews, coupons and more! Subscribe to our newsletter by visiting www.spearsbooks.org

Quantity Discounts: Spears Books are available at quantity discounts for orders of ten or more copies. Contact Spears Books at orders@spearsmedia.com.

Host a Reading Group: Learn more about how to host a reading group on our website at www.spearsbooks.org

www.ingramcontent.com/pod-product-compliance
Lightning Source LLC
Chambersburg PA
CBHW020853160426
43192CB00007B/906